CW00693023

THE HISTORY OF DROXFORD STATION
a journey through 1500 years

Pam Buttrey

© Pam Buttrey & Noodle Books (Kevin Robertson) 2012

ISBN 978-1-906419-93-6

First published in 2012

Produced by Noodle Books (Kevin Robertson) on behalf of Tony Williams - publisher.

NOODLE BOOKS PO Box 279, Corhampton, SOUTHAMPTON. SO32 3ZX

www.noodlebooks.co.uk

Printed in England by Ian Allan Printing.

Front cover - *The forecourt at Droxford probably not long after the railway opened. Was the conveyance awaiting a passenger perhaps or had arrived to collect parcels? The member of staff, possibly the station master Mr Wills, stands outside the entrance to the booking hall. On the other side of which a similar set of doors led on to the down platform.*

Tony Harden collection

Frontispiece - *A century later there are no more passengers and as a private residence its future is secure. Ironically it has now survived longer without passengers than it did with them, a better fate too than its neighbours at Wickham and West Meon both of which succumbed to demolition.* *Tony Williams*

Rear cover - *Droxford lives again. The rebuilt signal box at Droxford, completed in 2010, this now accommodates a guest suite over two levels. The building is a stunning recreation of the original which stood on the same spot. In keeping with its 21st century role insulation and consequently comfort is far better than was provided by the operating signal box - no draughts for example. There is no lever frame or signalling equipment. The windows - the window frames were copied from surviving window frames from the former Tisted signal box which still survive in that village as part of a garden shed - afford a superb panorama of the beautifully landscaped station area.* *Tony Williams*

CONTENTS

FOREWARD by TONY WILLIAMS

We had been house hunting for almost two years when my wife and I first viewed Old Droxford Station in October 2008. We knew after our first visit that it would be our new home and we duly moved in in March 2009. It is a fascinating property which was cleverly converted into a home by Mr and Mrs Olford in the mid 1980s. Their attention to detail was impressive, as too was the fact that they saved all the materials found on site. When we extended and updated the house and rebuilt the signal box all of these materials were put to good use. Recognising that we are the current guardians of this property we have tried to ensure that all of our works to the house and garden respect and enhance the integrity of the original design. The internet has helped us to source many materials and much memorabilia, from original LSWR barley twist lamp-posts to old photographs of the property.

I was keen to find out more about the history of Old Droxford Station and was lucky to meet people who had worked there, guarded it in the war and, as schoolchildren, taken the train either to school or to the cinema. I was also fortunate that many people, from local residents to archivists were prepared to retell their experiences and to lend me photographs and other materials, many of which have not been published before.

I commissioned Pam Buttrey to research and write the history. She has been meticulous in her research. I also asked Kevin Robertson, who is writing three books on the Meon Valley line, to edit the book and to assist with the photographs and layout. Both Pam and Kevin have done a first rate job and I am very grateful to them for their professionalism and support.

As this book shows, this site has had a life before and after the railway so perhaps in the future its walls will have even more stories to tell.

Tony Williams

Old Droxford Station

Extract from the Ordnance Survey 'one-inch' 1947 revision of Sheet 180 depicting the station at Droxford together with its proximity to Soberton and Brockbridge. Railway, river and road can be seen to all run in parallel, as indeed is the case for much of the Meon Valley.
Reproduced with kind permission of the Ordnance Survey

Abbreviations

OS	Ordnance Survey
TNA	The National Archives
HRO	Hampshire Record Office
VCH	Victoria County History

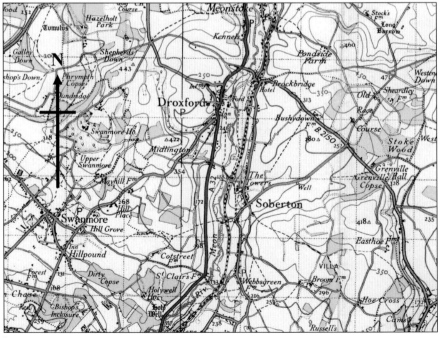

INTRODUCTION & ACKNOWLEDMENTS

Those of us who are 'of a certain age' remember, as children, standing on a railway platform waiting for the steam train to arrive. It 'chuffed' in, grey-black smoke turning white as it escaped into the air. Its elderly driver, having worked his way up to this important job, was assisted by the fireman shovelling coal into the fire hole to keep the engine going.

Those seeing people off, or waiting on the platform for relatives and friends, bought a one (pre-decimal) penny platform ticket. A porter, with navy blue cap and waistcoat, carried your luggage from or to the taxi, and was rewarded with a tip. Racing pigeons shuffled in piled willow crates on the platform, waiting to be released to fly home. In the sidings, an engine was taking on water from an elevated tank. Open bunkers of coal lay in the coal yard, where a coal merchant was based, since most homes had open fires.

On certain trains (although not it must be said not on the Meon Valley line), a sack of Royal Mail post was released mechanically into a net at the end of the platform as the train passed through, and picked up post. On mail trains, which carried passengers, postal staff sorted the post on board, dropping it off at major stations.

Many stations had a tea room, with strong British Railways tea served in British Railways china cups and saucers, with tea cakes and, perhaps, buttered toast. The station manager lived in the station house, and other staff in adjoining railway cottages.

Into the 1960s, and even with parents who had cars, students still travelled by train to and from college and university, their possessions in trunks collected by British Road Services' trucks, taken to the station, and carried by train. Parents did not yet transport their offspring and their luggage around the country.

In the mid-1950s, steam was replaced by diesel and electrification and, a decade later, many branch lines disappeared under Beeching but, the Meon Valley Railway was already axed – one of the last lines to be built, it was one of the first to close.

Visiting Droxford Station for the first time is a remarkable experience – to approach the frontage of an Edwardian house, and walk through the gates to the rear to discover a surviving platform with columns and the original canopy, another platform in front and, between the two platforms, a sunken area of grass where the track once lay!

Although little appears to have survived as a record of the construction of the track, bridges, tunnels etc, or the buildings, apart from initial plans and drawings of the route, surviving records show how the land was purchased, the impact of the railway on the local landscape and its population, and how the service altered over the years in response to national pressures and the public's attitude to trains.

My thanks are due to The National Archives, The House of Lords Record Office, Hampshire Record Office, the Sir Winston Churchill Archive Trust, the Society of Genealogists. Also the Bluebell Railway Museum, Hampshire Chronicle, Hampshire Field Club and Archaeological Society, Kidderminster Railway Museum, Mid Hants Railway, National Railway Museum, Soberton and Newtown Local History Society, South Western Circle, Stephenson Locomotive Society and the Transport Treasury.

Norman Buttery found additional details about Soberton and Droxford in trade directories, and Penny Smith tracked down an old Ordnance Survey map of the area, showing the railway track and stations, in a charity shop. Reg Daniels, Doris Gould and John Moon recalled memories of the station with Tony Williams, while Ann Pendred read the early draft and provided helpful additional information about Soberton and Droxford. Beryl Jackson allowed the use of postcards and photographs from the collection of the late Alan A. Jackson. Jeffrey Grayer shared his knowledge of the years immediately following the closure of the line, and read the draft for that period.

A number of individuals have also assisted, including, Pat Butler, Chris Cornell, Reg Daniels, Doris Gould, Tony Harden, John Moon, Colin Olford, Andrew Perrin, Chris Purdie, Annie Roseberry and of course Ray Stone. My apologies for anyone who has been omitted.

For the provision of maps I am grateful to Peter Swift, Peter Waller and Denis Tillman. Above all, I am indebted to Tony William's enthusiasm to discover more about Droxford Station's history.

Pam Buttrey, South Croydon, 2012.

The railway network of Hampshire and its associate environs almost at its peak. Taken from a contemporary map from the 1920s, a number of now long–lost lines are included. In Hampshire these include the lines to Lee-on-the-Solent, from Alton to Basingstoke, the branch to Bishops Waltham and from Hurstbourne to Fullerton. Even so some closures have already taken place, services from Gosport to Stokes Bay and Fratton to East Southsea both ceasing at the outbreak of WW1. Further closures would follow in the 1930s, although perhaps surprisingly some might say, the Meon Valley was not one of them. Its turn would come twenty years later in the next round. Even then this was not the end and more 'Last Day' specials would take place elsewhere through to 1973. Of note on the map is that the main lines, cross country routes and branches are by inference all of the same importance, junction stations where passengers might change for another route / service, are indicated by a rectangle against the location name.

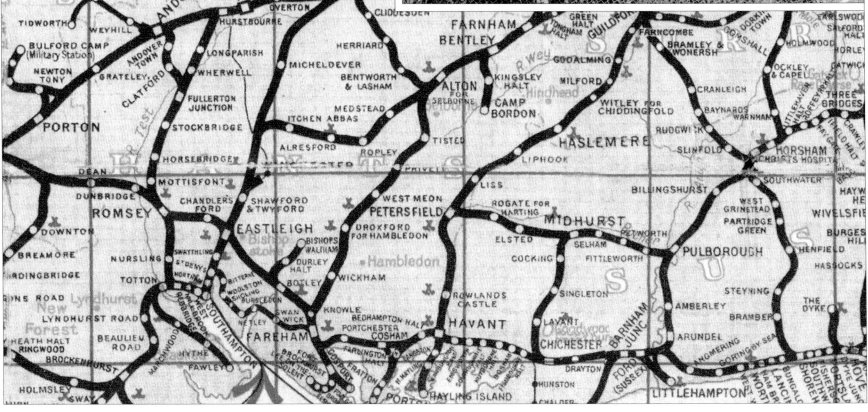

1
THE NEED FOR A RAILWAY?

On Sunday 6 February 1955 a special excursion train, with ten coaches drawn by two locomotives, left Waterloo carrying 530 passengers. As it steamed through Droxford Station at about 3.20 in the afternoon, people stood on both platforms to cheer it on its way[1]. All along the valley, small groups of people waved handkerchiefs from cottage windows or from the middle of fields[2].

At West Meon Station, there was a roaring trade at the ticket office as people bought single tickets to Privett and Droxford as souvenirs. They could never be used, the stop at West Meon being solely for the benefit of the locomotives to take on water whilst at the same time affording the enthusiasts the opportunity to take photographs. It was a final crumb of passenger revenue for British Railways from West Meon. The fact there would never be another passenger train from here to Droxford nor would the special be calling at Privett did not seem to matter, the tickets would now only be valuable as souvenirs.

The previous evening, the passenger train from Fareham to Alton had drawn into Droxford Station at 7.14 p.m. Despite it being a dark winter's night, some twenty people were there to greet it, and wave as it left. Giving a long whistle, it was soon on its way to West Meon[3]. The 6.48 p.m. train from Fareham, arriving at Alton at 7.43 p.m., was the last regular service passenger train to run on the Meon Valley Railway.

Opposite and right - *The special train of 6 February 1955 pauses at West Meon on its circular journey to and from Waterloo. The tour had taken in the Midhurst line which closed the same day. The views are taken from the road bridge which crosses the railway at the north end of West Meon station, the open carriage doors witness to the number of enthusiasts who wished to alight for photographs. Both locomotives were of the 'T9' class, affectionately known as 'Greyhounds' due to their speed. Once the pride of the London & South Western Railway and used on the fastest and most important services, as time passed they slowly descended on to lesser duties, which included passenger and, to a greater extent, freight workings over the Meon Valley line. In the right hand view the fireman of the rear engine may just be seen on top of the tender ready to refill the tank with water.*
Both: www.southern-images.co.uk

1. Stone, R.A., *The Meon Valley Railway*, (Southampton, 1983), pp. 95-9.
2. TNA, RAIL 1005/376: *Southern Daily Echo*.
3. Stone, *Meon Valley Railway*, p. 99.

Droxford and Soberton

Despite its name, Droxford Station was built just within the neighbouring parish of Soberton, close to the east bank of the River Meon in Hampshire. At this point, the Meon's flood plain is nearly 200 metres wide, the village of Droxford lying in a dry valley in gently sloping ground to the west. Its name derives from the Old English *drocen, ford*, perhaps a 'dry ford'[4].

The Meon Valley has, for centuries, provided a route upstream from the coast, and a home for those who chose to settle there. A pre-historic long barrow lies just south of Droxford village, and a Neolithic flint working site (OS SU616 183) and a Mesolithic site south-east of West Lodge (OS SU600 122) both in Soberton[5]. An Iron Age coin was found in 1881 (OS SU610 160).

Remains of a Roman building, north of Broom Farm in Soberton, may have been the centre of a large estate. Two large stone coffins from the Roman period were excavated in Brigden Coffin Field off Station Road (OS SU617 173), one of which now lies outside Soberton's parish church[6]. Later, invading Jutes moved upstream from the coast, establishing settlements along the Meon Valley[7]. A pagan cemetery, in use from in the late fifth century until about 600, was excavated on the site of Droxford Railway Station (see Chapters 2 and 6).

The diocese of Winchester was founded in 662 and, about 700, an administrative system of royal estates was set up, each with a minster church[8]. Droxford was one of the manors of the diocese of Winchester, the first known grant of land being in 826, when King Egbert, 'in gratitude to God for his coronation as king of all England', gave the vill of 'Drokeireford', with three mills, to the bishop of Winchester for 'the Sustenance of the Monks of Winchester'. Droxford became part of the Hundred of Waltham which, at first, was identical with the manor of Waltham which consisted of 38 hides acquired in 904 by the bishop of Winchester from King Edward the Elder, in exchange for 40 hides at Portchester[9]. In the Domesday Survey, Droxford remained part of the lands held by the bishop for the support of the monks of Winchester[10]. It passed to the bishop's use in 1284.

Part of the parish of Soberton, in the river valley north of Brockbridge, was transferred to Droxford in 1884. Droxford contained 6,937 acres until the tithings of Shidfield and Swanmore became separate parishes in 1894, leaving Droxford with 2,436 acres, its main crops being wheat, oats and barley, and some fruit. The village, lying along the main road from Fareham to Alton, close to and parallel with the river, contains many small Georgian houses as well as a large rectory and manor house. By 1895, there was a steam brewery and a flour mill. It was the administrative centre of the eleven parishes, including Soberton, which comprised the Droxford Poor Law Union, and the site of its workhouse.

Petty Sessions were held at the Court House in Droxford on alternate Thursdays; there was a police station, and the rural district council met once a month at the workhouse, where the superintendent registrar and his deputy were based. The Ecclesiastical Commissioners were lords of the manor, and there were four other large land owners. Both Droxford and Soberton had a post office, but the 'money order and telegraph office' was in Droxford.

Soberton

First recorded in the tenth century, the name of Soberton derives from the Old English *suth, bere-tun*: south barley farm/settlement [11]. The Domesday survey of 1086 recorded three large estates. William the Conqueror personally held a large part of Soberton, including three mills and three acres of meadow which would have been driven by water, formerly part of Earl Godwin's estates which King Harold added to the crown lands. Herbert the Chamberlain had three hides, including a mill, formerly held by Wulfnot, and Henry the Treasurer one hide, formerly held by Andrac. Durand held land in Soberton worth £11, formerly held by Alric and part of the manor of Old Alresford held by the Bishop of Winchester, and Earl Roger, a park consisting of a quarter of a hide[12].

4. http://www.nottingham.ac.uk/english/ins/kepn/detailpop.php?placeno=6628
5. The Neolithic long barrow would have been made between 4,500 and 2,400BC.
6. http://www.hants.gov.uk/hampshiretreasures/vol01/page253.html
7. Oppenheimer, S., *The Origins of the British*, (London, 2006, 2007 ed.), p. 360.
8. Yorke, Barbara, *Wessex in the Early Middle Ages*, (Leicester, 1995), p. 185.
9. *Victoria County History*, Hampshire and the Isle of Wight, ed. W. Page, 'Meonstoke Hundred', Miss F. Brough, (London, 1908), vol. 3, p. 274.
10. Williams, A. & Martin, G.H., eds., *Domesday Book*, (London, 2002), p. 99.
11. http://www.nottingham.ac.uk/english/ins/kepn/detailpop.php?placeno=6760
12. Williams & Martin, *Domesday Book*, pp. 90-1, 95, 118. *VCH*, vol. 3, p. 264: Soberton Mill in the south-west of the parish, worked by the Meon, and Rudley Mill in the south-east have survived

William Cobbett, in 1826, described Soberton Down as 'the *very greenest* thing I have seen in the whole country'. Estimating it at five or six hundred acres, he considered that

> The grass was *darker* than that of any pasture or even any sainfoin or clover that I have seen throughout the whole of my ride; and I should suppose that there could not have been many less than a thousand sheep in the three flocks that were feeding . . . [13]

In 1895, there were 5,871 acres in Soberton, the main crops being wheat and oats, with a number of small holdings in the south of the parish. Unlike Droxford, it had comprised a small village and a number of scattered settlements. A community developed at Newtown, in the south of the parish and, in 1850, it became a separate parish with a church built in 1851. With ten acres of glebe, its vicarage, in the patronage of the Bishop of Winchester, was worth £140 a year[14].

At the end of the nineteenth century, more houses were built in Soberton Heath and Chiphall. Homes, a church and shops were well established at Newtown, but there was little development at Brockbridge where Droxford Station would be built. Falkner John Minchin, Esquire, of Annagh in Tipperary and Holywell in Hampshire, was an absent lord of the manor, with four other principal landowners including Winchester College, known as 'The Warden and Scholars, Clerks of Saint Mary College, Winchester'.

The populations of both parishes increased in the nineteenth century. In 1801, Droxford contained about 1,200 people and Soberton 672 but both populations had almost doubled by 1871, after which they declined until the early twentieth century. In 1900, the road from Alton to Fareham ran through a sparsely populated agricultural area, with a string of villages providing for the needs of local people and travellers. There were many estates, with tenant farmers and agricultural labourers, and a number of large houses belonging to the gentry. Figure 1: The populations of Soberton and Droxford in the censuses from 1871 to 1931 The population of Droxford reduced after 1881 when the parish was divided up.

Today, Soberton has over 1500 inhabitants, following house-building in the parish. Droxford, with just over 600, has not grown since the 1960s.

YEAR	SOBERTON	DROXFORD
1871	1,245	2,325
1881	1,097	2,285
1891	1,185	532
1901	1,189	498
1911	1,302	572
1921	1,304	505
1931	1,336	505

Two carriers operated in Droxford in 1899: John Boswell traveled to Bishop's Waltham Railway Station whilst John Cousins, made a return journey to Southampton on Mondays, Portsmouth on Thursdays, passing through Soberton, and Winchester on Saturdays. As well as being a grocer, draper, ironmonger and wine merchant in Droxford, Mrs. Anne Clarke hired out horses and traps. Henry Hutton, a carrier in Soberton, made the return journey to Portsmouth on Tuesdays and Fridays [15]. Apart from these, people in the parish, rich and poor, depended on private or hired transport, or walked.

A railway in the valley

From 1851 onwards, there were several proposals to build a railway in the Meon Valley[16]. In 1860, the Petersfield Railway Company proposed to apply to Parliament for an Act which would include a junction in the tithing of Sheet, in Petersfield, and stations in some or all of the following: Sheet, Petersfield, Buriton and East Meon, West Meon, Warnford, Exton, Meonstoke, Corhampton, Droxford, Soberton, Bishop's Waltham, Durley, South Stoneham, Botley, Bishopstoke and Upham, terminating at a junction with the Gosport

13. Cobbett, William, *Rural Rides*, (1830, 2001 ed.), pp. 439-40. Dodd, J.P., *Proceedings of the Hampshire Field Club and Archaeological Society*, Hampshire Agriculture in 1853-4, vol. 35, 1979, pp. 239-60: they were probably Southdowns, first seen at Soberton in 1799, or a Southdown-Hampshire cross.

14. *VCH*, vol. 3, p. 274.

15. *Kelly's Directory*, 1899, p. 139, p. 420.

16. Tillman, Denis, *The Meon Valley Revisited*, (Bishops Waltham, 2003), p. 5.

branch of the London and South-Western Railway Company, hereafter known as the LSWR, in South Stoneham [17]. The following week, the LSWR applied for an Act to build the Petersfield and Botley Railway on the same route, but beginning eight hundred yards south of Petersfield Station, in the parish of Buriton [18].

In 1863, the Petersfield and Bishop's Waltham Railway proposed to apply to Parliament for an Act to build a railway from Bishop's Waltham to Petersfield, terminating just south of Petersfield Station with the Portsmouth branch of the LSWR, which would run from Bishop's Waltham through Droxford, Meonstoke, Exton, West Meon and East Meon [19].

The Havant, Hambledon and Droxford Railway, proposed in 1864 and 1865 by the Mid-Hampshire Railway Company, might have gone ahead, but they had second thoughts about constructing a line through sparsely populated country, and building a tunnel over a quarter of a mile long [20, 21]. In 1864, the Petersfield and Bishop's Waltham Railway was authorised: its track would run just north of Meonstoke Rectory. The Havant, Hambledon and Droxford Railway was intended to connect with it just north of where the road from Brockbridge to Bishop's Waltham crosses the A32. It would cross the River Meon close to Droxford Mill, running on the west side of the present Station Road, and then east to Hambledon [22].

Plans were altered and, in 1865, it was intended that the two railways would meet just north of Meonstoke Rectory. The line from Soberton would run over the rectory's gardens, lawns, pleasure ground, walks and shrubbery as well its pond, stream, meadow, osier beds and neighbouring glebe.

Glebe land had probably been given by one or more land owners in the centuries before the Reformation, usually in order to have prayers and masses said which would speed the way to Heaven for the donor and his family. Together with

tithes, the income from the glebe supplemented the priest's stipend and, until the sixteenth or early seventeenth century, he might have farmed it himself. In Meonstoke, the glebe was rented in 1865 by fifteen men, and was probably still strip-farmed. The railway would have taken some of Soberton's glebe, a field south of Brockbridge rented by Caleb Jackson [23]. No doubt the rector was grateful for objections to the private Bill: one was that the railway would 'anihilate [sic] the hunting' [24]. The plans did not materialise.

In 1881, the Windsor, Aldershot and Portsmouth Railway proposed a line beginning in Farnham, Surrey at a junction with the Guildford, Alton and Winchester line of the LSWR, and passing through Waverley, Frensham, Kingsley, Hartley Mauditt, Selborne, Newton Valence, to East Tisted and then down the Meon Valley through Droxford and Soberton, Hambleton, Catherington, Waterloo, Waterlooville, Southwick, Purbrook, Farlington, Widley, Wymering, Great Salterns, Landport, Southsea and Portsea, to Portsmouth, part of a network of railway lines proposed by the company [25].

None of the proposals went ahead so that, at a time when most communities now expected to be close to a railway line, there was none for an area in East Hampshire of some 30 to 35 miles from north to south and 17 to 20 miles from east to west. The LSWR lay on the north, east and west, and the London, Brighton and South Coast Railway, hereafter known as the LBSCR, along the south coast.

The Portsmouth, Basingstoke and Godalming Railway proposed an Act, in 1895, to provide several lines including one from Alton to Bedhampton, through Chawton and Faringdon and down the Meon Valley through Droxford, Soberton, Shedfield, Hambledon, Catherington, Barn Green, Waterloo, Stakes Green, Waterlooville, Farlington and Southwick [26].

17. *The London Gazette*, 23 November 1860, p. 4468.
18. *London Gazette*, 30 November 1860, p. 4861
19. *London Gazette*, 24 November 1863, p. 5814.
20. House of Lords RO, HL/PO/JO/1/777-8, HC/CL/PB/2/33/30.
21. TNA, RAIL 1005/376.
22. HRO, DP/245.
23. HRO, DP/264.
24. Tillman, *Meon Valley Revisited*, p.5.
25. *London Gazette*, 25 November 1883, p. 6131.
26. *London Gazette*, 22 November 1895, p. 6412.

In 1896, local landowners and other investors presented a Bill in Parliament for a main line railway from Basingstoke, where it would connect with the Great Western Railway, to Portsmouth, together with an east-west line from the Guildford area to near Alton. Most of the places which would have been connected by these routes were in predominately agricultural areas. According to *The Railway Magazine*, the land in the northern part was of poor quality and not very productive, so that the railway would be of little economic benefit, but the land would be cheap to purchase.

To distract the House of Lords' Committee from the fact that their prime purpose was to improve travel for landowners in the area, its promoters stressed its importance to the nation's defences, and the necessity for a direct route to Portsmouth, and its dockyard, from the north and east. Since the Napoleonic Wars, the army used heath land in north Hampshire for military training and, in 1892, established a balloon factory at Aldershot. The railway's promoters strongly insisted that it could only be run by the Great Western and South-Eastern Railways.

This was vigorously opposed by the LSWR and the LBSCR, who argued that Portsmouth was 'very adequately' served by three existing railways: it would be a waste of money to spend some £2,000,000 bringing two more railways to Portsmouth. After early disputes, the two companies had entered into joint arrangements for lines and stations in Portsmouth. The LSWR, which did not want to see the Great Western Railway encroaching eastwards into what it saw as its region, claimed that a light railway from Basingstoke to Fareham via Alton was sufficient, and undertook to construct it if the Committee would reject the Bill.

In 1897, the LSWR laid a Bill before Parliament proposing the construction of the Meon Valley Railway, almost 22½ miles in length between Alton Station, on their line between London and Winchester, and Fareham on a line belonging to the LBSCR, which ran south from London and then along the coast to Portsmouth. For most of its length, it would follow the course of the old London and Gosport turnpike road, now the A32. Having originally suggested a light railway, after meeting with the main landowners in the area, the LSWR's directors recommended to its shareholders that it should build a main line railway: 'a first-class railway with curves and gradients suitable for the passage of trains at express speed'[27].

The route would provide a train service from London via Aldershot, Alton and Fareham to Portsmouth, Gosport, Stokes Bay (for the Isle of Wight) and Southampton [28]. It would benefit the LSWR and the LBSCR's other interests for they jointly owned seven paddle steamers, between Portsmouth and Ryde and Stokes Bay and Ryde, and three horse-boats used for horses, carriages and other heavy traffic between Portsmouth and Stokes Bay and the Isle of Wight[29].

At Fareham, the line would connect with the Eastleigh to Gosport line, opened in 1840. It was hoped that Queen Victoria might use this route to go to Osborne House, which might have increased its popularity[30]. However, the military garrison consistently refused access to the waterfront at Gosport[31]. There was an expectation that Stokes Bay and Lee on the Solent would become popular resorts, which failed to happen [32, 33].

A railway at last!

In December 1896, two engineers, William R. Galbraith, the LSWR's consulting engineer, and E. Andrews estimated the total cost, including the widening of the route between Alton Station and Butts Junction, would be £399,500. 2s 3d. Henry Byers would be the resident engineer, the contract for its construction going to Messrs. Robert T. Relfe and Son of Plymouth. It included £4,000 to build five stations on the line at East Tisted, Privett (close to Basing Park), West Meon, Droxford and Wickham[34]. Mr. Thomas Phillips Figgis of London was appointed as architect of the stations and other building works.

27. *The Railway Magazine*, 'Extension of the London and South-Western Railway', vol. 12, (January to July 1903), pp. 499-505.
28. *London Gazette*, 20 November 1896, pp. 6424-5.
29. *The Railway Magazine*, 'The London and South-Western Railway's Steamers and Steamboat Services', John Bosham, vol. XII (January to July 1903), pp. 36-46. Simmons, J., & N. Biddle, N., eds., *The Oxford Companion to British Railway History*, (Oxford 1997, 1999 ed.), p. 286: The two companies jointly owned two miles of line at Ryde on the Isle of Wight.
30. Stone, *Meon Valley Railway*, p. 25.
31. Stone, *Meon Valley Railway*, p. 34.
31. Robertson, Kevin, *Hampshire Railways in Old Photographs*, (Gloucester, 1989), p. 109.
32. http://en.wikipedia.org/wiki/Meon_Valley_Railway
33. D:\SWC Meon Valley Portfolio R9D\reasons02.htm
34. Stone, *Meon Valley Railway*, pp. 8-11. Buttrey, Pam, *Lyss Place: Peace and Turmoil for the Gentry in Liss from 900AD*, (South Croydon, 2008), pp. 338-40: The Basing Park estate was owned by William Nicholson, the largest landowner in Hampshire whose family's fortune came from the manufacture of gin.

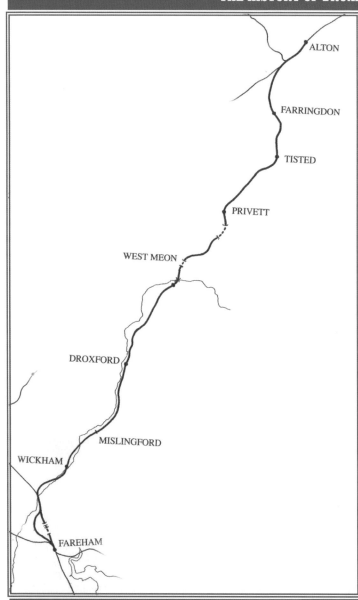

The route of the Meon Valley Railway.
Courtesy of Denis Tillman.

'The South Western (Meon Valley) Railway Act', passed on 3 June 1897, empowered the LSWR to purchase land and to construct the Meon Valley Railway[35]. Earlier that year, the Company was authorised to construct a light railway, 12½ miles long, between Basingstoke Station and Butts Bridge. Built through 'the northern, or poorer district', it opened in June 1901, proving a good service 'of more advantage to landowners than to the railway company'.

As the LSWR's prime aim now was a main line service between London and the Hampshire coast, they would first build a double track from Alton to Butts Bridge where the Meon Valley Railway began. Although the Meon Valley line was single track, its tunnels, viaduct, overbridges and most of the underbridges were to be constructed for a double track, with a gauge of 4 foot 8½ inches, which could be built in the future by widening the cuttings and embankments.

There would be double tracks at each station, the platforms being 600 feet long to provide for long main line trains. The railway lines were to be of the heaviest standard type used by the LSWR. In the opinion of the author of an article in *The Railway Magazine* in 1903, the engineering works were 'exceedingly expensive'. At the northernmost section, water was scarce which meant sinking deep wells and, for the first 17 miles from Butts Bridge, brick earth, building sand and clean gravel had to be brought in at a very great cost. South of Droxford, the railway entered the Reading Beds which made construction difficult.

The LSWR, who believed that it would be a profitable link with the Hampshire coast and the Isle of Wight, were dependent on the support of local landowners. *The Railway Magazine* observed that:

The Meon Valley Railway passes through a beautiful residential and sporting district, and the line will be of very great convenience and value to the landowners[36].

There was a depression in agriculture in the last quarter of the nineteenth century, with a fall in the price of corn and wheat, and it was an opportunity for some to make money by selling land to the LSWR. For Winchester College, in Soberton, it included part of the River Meon, three fields and a stream. Mr. Falkner John Minchin sold land in Soberton and Droxford, including twenty-two fields, and the River Meon and its banks[37].

Now that the LSWR would definitely go ahead with plans to build a railway along the Meon

35. TNA, RAIL 1066/1708: *60-61 Victoria cap.35 1897*.
36. *The Railway Magazine*, 'Extension of the London and South-Western Railway', vol. XII (January to July 1903), pp. 499-505.
37. HRO, DP 515/1-2.

valley, an extraordinary general meeting was held by liquidators at the Town Hall in Portsmouth on 8 December 1898, in order to wind up one of the unsuccessful proposals, named the Portsmouth, Meon Valley and Alton Railway Extension Company Limited[38].

That same year, the Bishop's Waltham Light Railway applied to the Light Railway Commissioners to construct, maintain and work a light railway between Bishop's Waltham and the Meon Valley near Brockbridge. It would run from a junction with the LSWR's railway at Bishop's Waltham, immediately opposite the north end of the passenger platform, passing through the parishes or places of Swanmore, Droxford, Soberton, Meonstoke and Corhampton, to a junction with the Meon Valley Railway 'at a point 10 yards, or thereabouts, measured along that railway in a south-westerly direction from the centre of the road leading from Brock Bridge to Hambledon'. The gauge would be 4 foot 8½ inches and the power steam, electricity 'or other mechanical power'[39]. The Light Rail Commissioners submitted an Order made by them for its construction to the Board of Trade[40]. After modification, it was confirmed by the Board of Trade on 1 November 1900, but was never constructed[41].

38. *London Gazette*, 27 December 1898, p. 8364.
39. *London Gazette*, 23 May 1899, pp. 3263-4.
40. *London Gazette*, 20 February 1900, p. 1180.
41. *London Gazette*, 2 November 1900, p. 6696.

What might have been, the 1900 Bishops Waltham to Droxford (Brockbridge) Light Railway. In reality the sparsely populated countryside, allied to the need for heavy engineering, rendered the proposal unrealistic from the outset. Courtesy of Andrew Perrin

LIGHT RAILWAYS ACT, 1896.

BISHOP'S WALTHAM LIGHT RAILWAY ORDER, 1900.

ORDER

MADE BY THE

LIGHT RAILWAY COMMISSIONERS,

AND MODIFIED AND CONFIRMED BY THE

BOARD OF TRADE,

AUTHORISING THE CONSTRUCTION OF A

LIGHT RAILWAY IN THE COUNTY OF SOUTHAMPTON, FROM BISHOP'S WALTHAM TO A JUNCTION WITH THE AUTHORISED MEON VALLEY RAILWAY NEAR BROCK BRIDGE IN THE PARISH OF SOBERTON.

Presented to both Houses of Parliament by Command of His Majesty.

LONDON:
PRINTED FOR HIS MAJESTY'S STATIONERY OFFICE,
BY DARLING & SON, LTD., 34–40, BACON STREET, E.

And to be purchased, either directly or through any Bookseller, from
EYRE & SPOTTISWOODE, EAST HARDING STREET, FLEET STREET, E.C., and
32, ABINGDON STREET, WESTMINSTER, S.W.; or
JOHN MENZIES & CO., ROSE STREET, EDINBURGH, and
90, WEST NILE STREET, GLASGOW; or
HODGES, FIGGIS & CO., LIMITED, 104, GRAFTON STREET, DUBLIN.

1901.

[Cd. 475.]   *Price 2½d.*

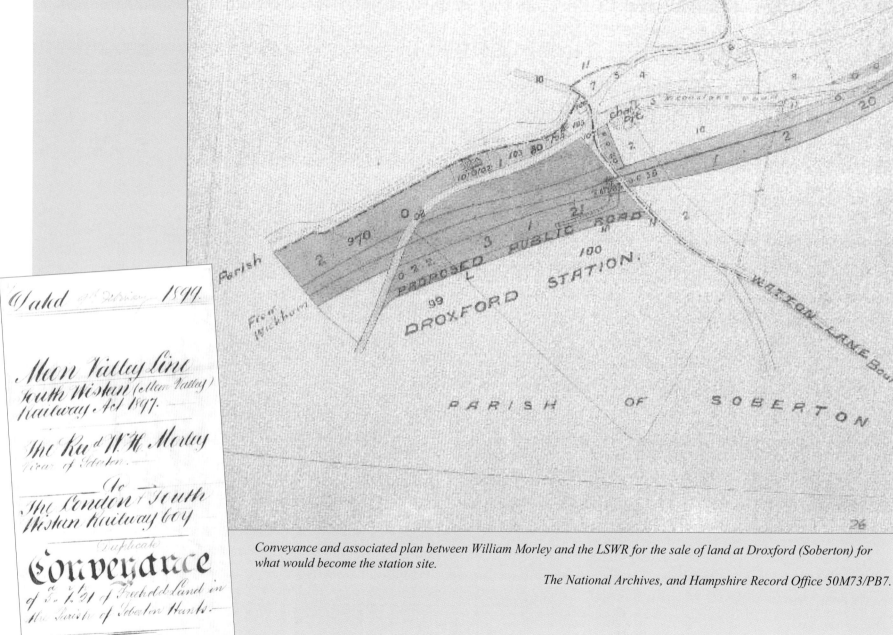

Conveyance and associated plan between William Morley and the LSWR for the sale of land at Droxford (Soberton) for what would become the station site.

The National Archives, and Hampshire Record Office 50M73/PB7.

14

2
BUYING THE LAND

The LSWR produced detailed plans of the proposed route of the railway, and the sites of the stations. As Brockbridge was close to a bridge crossing the River Meon, it was the obvious choice for a station accessible to the residents of nearby Droxford, the local administrative centre, as well as Soberton, Hambledon and other settlements in the district. Despite being in the parish of Soberton, it was called Droxford Station in the design stage, probably as Droxford was a larger and more prosperous village in a parish where several 'gentry' family lived.

Five houses stood in Brockbridge, close to the road leading to the bridge. Four roads and a lane met there one of which, from Soberton village, would be realigned to pass in front of the station, and renamed as Station Road. Meonstoke Road led from Meonstoke, and a lane from the ford at Droxford Mill. The main road, Hatton Lane, went to Hambledon, a large village, after a smaller road forked off to Clanfield. Droxford Station's platform signs would describe it as 'Droxford for Hambledon'.

The Glebe

Droxford Station would be built on field No. 100 at Brockbridge which, with field No. 97, was part of forty acres of glebe in Meonstoke and Soberton, 'in the gift of the Bishop of Winchester', held by the rector of Meonstoke (see opposite) [1]. When parishes were established, probably in the tenth century, Soberton was probably in the parish of Meonstoke.

The oldest part of Soberton's church may have been built before the Norman Conquest, having similar dimensions to the Anglo-Saxon church at Boarhunt which dates from about 1064. A north aisle was added to Soberton church's nave about 1200 [2]. As it was a chapel of ease attached to Meonstoke Church, there is no mention of a church in Soberton in the Domesday Survey [3]. The earliest record of a chapel in Soberton was in 1284 when Edward I quitclaimed the advowson of the church in Meonstoke, with a chapel annexed to it, to the bishop of Winchester [4]. In 1291, the church in Meonstoke and the chapel were assessed at £33. 6s 8d [5].

In a glebe terrier for 1696, the 'parsonage' of Meonstoke had thirty-three acres, of which ten acres were arable land in the parish of Soberton [6]. There were thirteen acres of glebe in Soberton in 1859, while field No. 100 comprised thirteen acres and seventeen perches in 1899 [7,8].

William Hammond Morley came to Soberton in 1874, as 'curate in sole charge of Soberton' to the seventy-five year old rector of Meonstoke, the Reverend Charles John Hume. William was the last of a long line of curates in Soberton. The seventh of eleven children, although two died young, he was born in late 1843 to George Morley, vicar of Newport Pagnell in Buckinghamshire, and his wife Martha Rebecca.

George, whose father was the Reverend John Morley, vicar of Aylesbury, went to Cambridge University in 1826 and became vicar of Newport Pagnell in 1832

1. Gelling, Margaret, *Place-Names in the Landscape*, (London 1984, 2000 ed.), pp. 17-8. Brockbridge derives from the OE *brōc*, 'brook, stream', a word not found in use before 730, and would mean a bridge over a stream or brook; *Kelly's Directory*, Hampshire, 1895, p. 425.
2. *Victoria County History*, Hampshire and the Isle of Wight, ed. W. Page, 'Meonstoke Hundred', Miss F. Brough, (London, 1908), vol. 3, p. 267; http://www.earlybritishkingdoms.com/adversaries/bios/wilfredpt2.html: St. Wilfred the Elder (634-709), the Bishop of York, was exiled from Northumbria in 680. According to Bede, he settled in Sussex where he converted its occupants, and the Jutes or Meonwaras in the Meon Valley, to Christianity before going to the Isle of Wight in 685.
3. Williams, A. & Martin, G.H., eds, *Domesday Book*, (London, 2002), p. 96.
4. *VCH*, vol. 3, p. 257.
5. *VCH*, vol. 3, p. 267: There was another chapel in Soberton, sited in Hoe: a dispute arose between Roger, lord of Hoe, and the rector of Meonstoke and parishioners of the chapel, which was referred to the bishop in 1282.
6. HRO, 21M65/E15/82.
7. Lewis, Samuel, *Topographical Dictionary of England*, vol. 4, (London, 1859), p. 129.
8. TNA, RAIL 411/408 .
9. J. A. Venn, *Alumni Cantabrigienses*, Part 2 1752-1900, vol 4 (Cambridge, 1951). His wife was born Martha Rebecca Dawson at Great Hale, Lincolnshire in 1811.

until his death there in 1865[9]. In the 1851 census, a governess, cook and two housemaids lived in his household, and three servants were there ten years later [10]. George Morley was no poverty-stricken clergyman for he left nearly £40,000. His father, John Morley, came from Elworthy in Somerset, where their ancestors were clergyman there and earlier in North Petherton, going back to the early 1600s.

William became a student at Worcester College, Oxford in 1863 at the age of seventeen, and graduated with a B.A. in 1867. He became a curate at Snitterfield in Warwickshire in 1869 and obtained an M.A. from Worcester College two years later[11]. He appears in the 1871 census as a curate lodging in Snitterfield, while his widowed mother and four sisters lived eight miles away at Milverton, near Leamington Spa[12]. His mother died in September 1871, leaving under £3,000. Despite having three older brothers, William proved both of his parents' wills.

In 1878, William Morley lived in Droxford[13]. He married Mary Sophia Johns in April 1878 at St. Saviour's Church in Southwark, now Southwark Cathedral. Some twelve years younger than William, she was born in Southwark in 1855, a daughter of the Reverend Bennett Johns who ran 'The School for the Indigent Blind', a large residential school for boys and girls in St. George's Street, Southwark. In the 1871 census, she was the eldest of four children living with their recently widowed father, her youngest sister being eight months old[14].

William and Mary lived at Eden Lodge in Droxford in the 1881 census, with their two year old daughter, Mary Rebecca, a cook and housemaid[15]. Ten years later, they were in the 'Parsonage' in Soberton, today known as Soberton House, close to St Peter's Church. Mary Rebecca 12 and Violet Martha 8, had a governess, and there were two domestic servants. Their son, Norbert, also eight

years old, was probably away at school[16]. Earlier curates only stayed a short time, but William Morley found Soberton's old church 'in a deplorable condition' and resolved to amend its plight, beginning an enormous restoration programme after an appeal to raise £1,800 [17]. It was completed in 1881 at a cost of £2,000, and its tower the same year[18]. The latter cost £113, said to been given by local servants, having been originally built with a bequest from a butler and his wife, a dairymaid, who had no children[19]. Edna Rainsley described William as a man who 'clearly loved the people . . . A man of humanity and education, with undoubted status, he assumed the mantle of leadership'[20]. William's second appeal circular began with this request: 'Will you kindly send a little help to a very poor Agricultural Parish? Having no resident Gentry, we can only hope . . .'. It may not have endeared him to the Twynhams of Soberton House, the leading family in the parish[21].

William Morley had sufficient income, inherited from his father, to remain as a curate in Soberton, with servants, and to pay for his children's education. He did not leave a will but three brothers did: John Lacy Morley left £22,914 in 1907 while Edward Dawson Morley, who also remained a curate for many years, left £7,280 in 1917 and Alexander Lacy Yea Morley left £16,456 in 1925[22].

Rectors of Meonstoke had opposed suggestions that Soberton should be separate as they did not want to lose the income from Soberton's tithes, which were much larger than those of Meonstoke. The Reverend Charles Hume was a son of Abraham Hume of Bilston Grange, near Rugby, in Warwickshire. Born about 1798-9 he became rector of Meonstoke in 1832[23]. Unlike Morley, he was not a wealthy man. When he died in July 1893, aged ninety-five and still rector of Meonstoke, he left £1,583.

10. TNA, HO107/1723/415; RG9/873/63.
11. J. Foster, *Alumni Oxonienses 1500-1714*, vol. 3, (London, 1891); J. Foster, *Alumni Oxonienses 1715-1886*, vol. 3, (London, 1888).
12. TNA, RG10/3206/84; RG10/3196/107.
13. *White's Gazetteer and Directory of the County of Hampshire etc.*, 1878, p. 509.
14. TNA, RG10/606/24
15. TNA, RG11/1238/67.
16. TNA, RG12/943/111.
17. Edna Rainsley, *Soberton Stories – Number One: William Hammond Morley M.A. Curate and Vicar of the Parish 1874 to 1920*, (Soberton, 1974).
18. *Kelly's Directory*, Hampshire, 1899, p. 420.
19. *Kelly's Directory*, Hanpshire, 1895, p. 425.
20. Rainsley, *Morley*.
21. Information from Ann Pendred
22. National Probate Index; Edward Dawson Morley: see Foster, *Alumni Oxonienses 1715-1886*, vol. 2.
23. Foster, *Alumni Oxonienses 1715-1886*, vol. 2; Venn, *Alumni Cantabrigienses*, Part 2 1752-1900, vol. 3 (Cambridge, 1951).

Hume was succeeded by the Reverend Canon James Richard Philip Hoste B.A., a canon of Winchester Cathedral, who was rector of Meonstoke from 1893 until his death in 1897[24]. In May 1897, St. Peter's Church in Soberton eventually became a church in its own right and, in November, the Reverend William Hammond Morley M.A. was 'collated to the New Vicarage of Soberton'[25].

As a chapelry annexed to Meonstoke Rectory, in 1895 the joint gross annual value was £841[26]. Morley's annual salary as a curate is not known but, in 1899 as rector, the living of Soberton was worth £480 a year gross[27].

The Sale

The early plans show that considerable leeway was made for the final position of the railway. Although a central line was shown, allowance was made for the outer edge of the railway to be up to 400 feet (about 120 metres) either side of this central line. At Droxford Station, the completed railway kept close to the original central line[28]. This was determined by June 1898 when Mr Charles R. Gunner of Messrs Gunner and Penny, of Bishop's Waltham and Portsmouth, commenced as the Reverend William Morley's solicitor and informed the LSWR's solicitors, Messrs. Bircham & Company, that it was glebe land[29].

This meant a Bill in the Chancery Division between the vicar of Soberton, as 'owner without power of sale', and the LWSR to permit the sale of the glebe, under the provisions of the Lands Clauses Consolidation Act 1845[30]. In November, Mr Gunner informed Bircham & Company that Mr Morley wanted the money from the sale, which would be paid into the Court of Chancery, to be used to build a 'Parsonage' in Soberton. Bircham & Company would try to meet his wishes and, in January 1899, they asked for proof of Mr Morley's induction as rector[31].

Mr Morley made an agreement with the LSWR on 22 November 1898 (see illustration page 14), for the sale of 3 acres, 1 rod and 21 perches in field No. 100, and 2 acres in field No. 97[32]. In January 1899, Mr Gunner was dealing with the conveyance, and the nomination of a surveyor to check the valuation of the land prior to completion. Mr Morley signed the nomination but not the conveyance, since it 'did not provide for some of the necessary accommodation works'[33]. The LSWR agreed to plant and maintain a quickset hedge on the south side of the new Station Road, where it ran alongside field No. 100, and to erect a temporary fence until the hedge was thoroughly established. It would provide new convenient means of access into fields Nos. 97 and 100, with proper gradients, shifting the existing gates to the new entry ways, and ensure that Mr Morley was 'reasonably' satisfied[34].

On 27 January, the agreement was made to nominate 'two able practical surveyors', John Arthur Wallington of Basing for the LSWR and John Henry Appleby of Fareham for Mr Morley, to determine together if the agreed purchase price of £425 was accurate, taking into account that the railway would divide the glebe. They confirmed, on 31 January, that it was 'the proper and full value'[35]. In October 1901, Mr Appleby, of Newman and Appleby of Fareham, would be paid £13. 2s 6d by the LSWR for acting on behalf of Mr Morley, having visited Soberton in 1897 and 1898 to value the land and 'to see that the frontage to the new Road was properly secured', settling the compensation at £425 and corresponding with them regarding the 'Road frontage'[36].

The Bill continued in Chancery and, on 24 January, Mr Gunner visited Soberton's postmaster, Alexander Day Holmes, whom he described as 'between 80 and 90 and very infirm'[37]. Aged 85, Mr. Holmes made a declaration that he had lived in Soberton for 62 years, and was assistant overseer of the parish for

24. *Kelly's Directory*, 1895, p. 425. This included glebe in Meonstoke.
25. HRO, H/CL7/174/5.
26. *Kelly's Directory*, Hanpshire, 1895, p. 425. *Kelly's Directory*, Hampshire, 1899, p. 420.
27. TNA, RAIL 411/408; HRO, DP/515/1.
28. HRO, H/CL7/174/7.
29. HRO, H/LL7/174/4.
30. HRO, H/CL7/174/7.
31. HRO, H/CL7/174/2.
32. HRO, H/CL7/174/7.
33. HRO, H/CL7/174/7.
34. HRO, 50M93/PB7.
35. HRO, H/CL7/174/3.
36. HRO, H/CL7/174/9.
37. HRO, H/CL7/174/7.

all but the last four years of that period[38]. He had always known that the lands which Mr Morley had contracted to sell to the LSWR formed part of the glebe lands of the parish of Soberton, and that the vicar was entitled to its rents and profits[38]. On 31 January, Mr Gunner witnessed and took away Mr Holmes' declaration, paying him 10s, and witnessed Mr Morley's signing of the conveyance[39].

The completion took place on 9 February 1899, the purchase money having been paid into the Court of Chancery the previous day. Mr Morley was asked to detail his expenses and, on 20 February, the Court decided his costs at £2.19s 8d [40]. He paid tithe and land taxes on the sale. On 28 March, Gunner & Penny received a cheque for their fee of £20. 12s 10d from Bircham & Company. (See conveyance illustration page 14)[41].

William Morley and his successors would benefit from living in a new rectory. On 5 June 1899, Mr. Minchin, lord of the manor, sold land adjacent to the church and the White Lion for the site of a 'parsonage', while the Governor of Queen Anne's Bounty for the Augmentation of the Maintenance of Poor Clergy provided a mortgage of £2,200 to build the house[42]. In the 1901 census, aged 57, he lived in the Rectory next to the church with Mary, their daughter Mary Rebecca 21, son Norbert 18 and a cook and parlour maid, two young sisters born in Gosport[43].

His wife Mary Sophia died on 14 October 1913, aged 58, at The Nursing Home in Winchester, leaving £78. 8s 9d, while William remained as rector until his retirement in 1920, aged seventy six. When he died on Easter Day, 12 April 1925, aged eighty-one years, he was buried with his wife in Soberton's churchyard.

Change at Brockbridge

When the glebe was sold, field No. 100 was leased to a tenant farmer, Thomas Christian of Bushy Down Farm, aged about 55; he and his wife were both born in Lincolnshire. Another seven fields of the farm, belonging to Mr. Minchin, would likewise be reduced in size by the construction of the railway[44]. On 24 May, Thomas Christian, as tenant of field No. 100, received £248. 3s 4d compensation and, on 26 May, William Davis had £38 compensation as tenant of field No. 97[45].

The station's sidings and goods yard would be cut into the gardens of plots 101 and 102 owned by Laura Annie Williams, born locally about 1864, and Sarah Williams [46]. Harriett Hatch lived in the house at plot No.101, and Sarah Williams at plot No. 102. Plot No.103, a garden with outbuildings belonging to Laura Annie and Sarah Williams, was occupied by Harriett Hatch and Sarah Williams. The original road to Soberton would be diverted slightly to the west, providing access to the goods yard, and occupy plot No. 103 and part of plot No. 104, a garden and outbuildings owned by James Westbrook and rented by James Varndall. The plots numbered 105 and 106, houses owned by James Westbrook, were occupied by William Sheppard and James Varndall respectively[47].

In the 1901 census, William Sheppard, aged about 39, was born in Droxford and his wife in Soberton, their five children, aged from 14 to 5, all being born in Brockbridge. Sheppard, as a house painter and glazier, would probably benefit from the building of new houses in Station Road following the opening of the railway. His neighbour, James Varndall aged about 67, was a general labourer while his wife Catherine worked at home as a laundress. Anne Samways, 21 and born in Droxford, lived with them, being employed as a laundry maid[48].

On 9 January 1899, James Westbrook conveyed plot No. 104, copyhold land containing 10 perches, for £50 and, on 1 May 1899, Miss Laura A. Williams conveyed the plots numbered 101, 102 and 103, comprising 1 rod and 30 perches, and received £500. Varndall received £3 compensation as tenant of the garden at plot No. 101. All four plots, part of the manor of Soberton, were enfranchised on 11 October 1901[49]. There would soon be great changes to the landscape at Brockbridge.

38. HRO, H/LL7/174/4.
39. HRO, H/CL7/174/7.
40. HRO, H/CL7/174/6, HRO, H/CL7/174/8.
41. HRO, H/CL7/174/7.
42. Rainsley, *Morley*.
43. TNA, RG13/1090/98.
44. HRO, DP 515/1-2.
45. TNA, RAIL 411/408. In a deed dated 26 May 1899, the Rev. W.H. Morley received £38 for plot 97.
46. In several editions of *Kelly's Directory*, Miss Laura Anne Williams, R.A.M., of Vincent Cottage in Droxford, was a professor of music and an organist.
47. HRO, DP 515/1.
48. TNA, RG13/1090/99.
49. TNA, RAIL 411/408.

3
BUILDING THE RAILWAY

Construction began from the Alton end of the line. Navvies cleared the land with picks and shovels. In 1900, in the *Church Times*, Canon Benham described the scene, probably near to his home village of West Meon, where he saw great chalk embankments: 'There are cuttings through the rising ground, and a vast amount of chalk is brought forth to level up the valley beyond'. He watched 'big carts coming out of the cuttings and along the chalk road already constructed' which 'at a given point wheeled round, shot their load out onto the heap, and went back for more'[1]. Gunpowder was probably used to break up the chalk in the cutting, the work often done by miners from Devon and Cornwall[2]. A photograph taken near Droxford shows a large steam shovel loading chalk onto carts[3]. Messrs Robert T. Relf & Son used at least eight small steam engines, as well as cranes and excavators[4].

Human remains

In late June and in July 1900, the *Hampshire Chronicle* reported a 'improved roadway' from Droxford to the proposed new railway station at Brockbridge. Work began to construct the railway through Soberton. Immediately north of the site of the station, the line was carried on a bridge across the road and, where the station would be built, it entailed digging a cutting through the top of a spur of high ground which rose steeply from the floor of the Meon valley.

In the summer of 1900, Mr W. Dale, F.S.A (Fellow of the Society of Antiquaries), of 5 Sussex Place, Southampton, visited the site on several occasions, being informed that human bones had been found there, some covered with big flints, as well as spearheads and pieces of 'much corroded metal'. He took away some spearheads, battered fragments of iron and smaller objects. As the Meon Valley was known to have been occupied by Jutes, he presumed that the finds were Jutish. Reporting his finds in a paper to the Society of Antiquaries on 15 May, 1902, Mr Dale explained that:

Very little progress was made with the railway in 1900, owing to the scarcity of

Construction south of Droxford. Wagons would be placed alongside the 'steam navvy' and removed. There would then be a short break in proceedings - as here - whilst further rail wagons were pushed into place. The excavator moving a few feet forward under its own power when required.
David Foster-Smith collection

1. Stone, R.A., *The Meon Valley Railway*, (Southampton, 1983), p. 34.
2. Coleman, Terry, *The Railway Navvies*, (London, 1965), pp. 44-5, p. 196.
3. Aldsworth, F., *Proceedings of the Hampshire Field Club and Archaeological Society*, 'Droxford Anglo-Saxon Cemetery, Soberton, Hampshire', vol. 35, 1979, p. 98.
4. Robertson, Kevin, *Hampshire Railways in Old Photographs*, (Gloucester, 1989), p. 96.

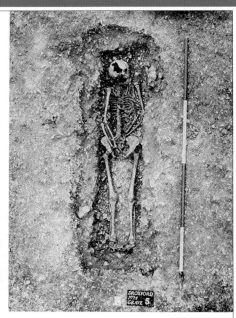

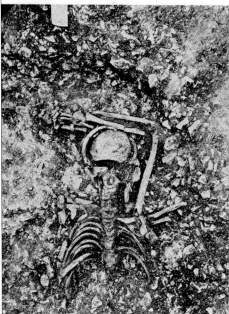

labour, and the cutting, after going about halfway through the field where the interments were, stopped until last autumn, when the work was again resumed and fresh discoveries made. The place is 20 miles from my home and 5 miles from any station, but I managed to go once or twice every week and was present on several occasions when burials were struck. I was also fortunate in enlisting the help of a couple of navvies who were more intelligent than is usual with their class, and who had a keen eye for business, so that I have been able to obtain almost everything of any importance[5].

The later excavation of the site in 1974 suggested that the bones which he found in the summer of 1900 were in an area immediately south of the station building, and that work halted in 1900 south of where the railway track would cross the road.

On 25 August 1900, an application was made to build a new hotel at Brockbridge, near to the proposed station, 'if the light railway comes . . .'. The Railway Hotel, later renamed as the Station Hotel, opened the following year, after the census on 31 March 1901. In October 1901, a road was being built 'from the bottom of Garson Hill to the new station at Brockbridge', but there is little information about the area where the station was sited.

Dale wrote in 1906 that:

'After the main cutting was completed . . . the railway was widened a little near the station and . . . a few more things were found'. In January 1902, the local committee of the Meon Valley Navvy Mission was dissolved 'as the cuttings are nearly finished'[6].

*Left - The Droxford anglo-saxon cemetery. **Top left**: warrior grave, **top right**: 'coffin' grave', **below left**: female grave, **below right**: graves classified 'Nos 16 and 17'. (See pages 86 and 88-90).*
From Hampshire Field Club and Archaeological Society, vol 35 (1978)

5. Dale, W., *Proceedings of the Society of Antiquaries*, 'On the discovery of an Anglo-Saxon cemetery at Droxford', vol. 9, pp. 125-9.
6. Aldsworth, F., *Pros. Hants. Field Club & Arch.. Soc.* vol. 35, pp. 93-182. It includes this quote from *The Hampshire Chronicle*, 19 October 1901.

The burials were close to the surface in 'a tenacious clayey earth', although the ground gave no indication of what lay below. It was difficult to remove anything of any size whole, and skulls could only be removed in fragments. Teeth were 'perfect and well-preserved'. Mr Dale described the cemetery as:

> ". . confined to the top of the hill, and the railway cut through about 100 yards of it north to south. It no doubt extended further east and west in the ground not touched by the railway. The interments were numerous and close together".

The finds included thirty-two spearheads, eight shield bosses, swords, two Roman coins, a gilt bronze pendant, glass beads which probably formed necklaces, tweezers, spindles, whorls and two wooden buckets hooped with bronze bands. There were saucer-shaped concave brooches similar to those found in Jutish settlements in Kent[7]. Dale's original notes have not survived; only two published descriptions remain, given in 1902 and 1906. He donated at least 176 objects to the British Museum, and 27 to Winchester City Museum. Remains of four skeletons, including four mandibles, parts of two skulls, and a femur, went to the Royal College of Surgeons until 1951 and 1955, and then to the Natural History Museum. They belonged to a woman, probably aged nearly thirty, a man nearly fifty years old and two young men aged about twenty[8].

The Navvies

Although Dale suggested that no work took place between the summer of 1900 and the autumn of 1901, the census taken on 31 March 1901, lists 67 men living in Soberton and 2 in Droxford who were working on the railway. Without the influx of railway workers and their families into the parish, the population of Soberton would have dropped: there were 1,185 inhabitants in 1891 and 1,189 in 1901.

The occupations given indicate that a working track had been laid down. Most of the men were railway navvies but there were three foremen, a ganger plate worker, two plate layers, two platers, an engine driver, a 'worker in railway engine', a 'steam engine, maker, fitter' and a stoker, as well as a fencer, a 'horse hirer' and two carters. Two Church Army evangelists, John B. Thompson 25 and his visitor James Barclay 20, lived in Down Road.

A typical navvy / family hut. These were very much temporary affairs and were erected at a number of 'centres' along the course of the route. Certainly on the Meon Valley line, this one was probably near Privett. Besides affording accommodation for at least one married man and family, the huts accommodated a number of single men.   *David Foster-Smith collection*

Twenty-eight men were born in Hampshire, including fourteen already living in Soberton, the majority being young men described as navvies. An exception was Frank Lindsay 17, the 'steam engine, maker, fitter' whose father was the schoolmaster. Most lived with their parents, such as George Winsor 17, whose father was innkeeper at 'The Falcon' in Horns Hill, Richard Cleere 14, son of William Cleere who ran the 'Royal Oak Inn', and Charles Janaway 27 of the Kiln, Soberton Heath, whose father was a labourer. The contractors paid better wages and the likelihood is that, without the railway, they would have been agricultural labourers who, with the depression in agriculture, were increasingly employed on a casual basis as day labourers[9]. According to Kenneth Ward, six hundred labourers were employed, earning 6d an hour[10].

7. Dale, W., *Proceedings of the Society of Antiquaries*, vol. 9, pp. 125-9,
8. Aldsworth, F., *Pros. Hants Field Club & Arch. Soc.* vol. 35, pp. 93-182.
9. Stone, *Meon Valley Railway*, p. 22. According to R. A. Stone, local landowners in West Meon were fearful that local wages would rise. They threatened families in tied cottages with eviction if sons worked on the railway, so railway workers moved in with relatives. This does not appear, from the 1901 census, to have been the case in Soberton.
10. Kenneth Ward, *Droxford in the Meon Valley*, (Havant).

The construction of the main station building at Droxford. As with the other stations on the line, it would provide living accommodation for the station master and his family. Each of the stations on the Meon Valley were 'handed', meaning the private accommodation was either at the left or right hand end. The choice depended upon the position of the station building relative to the approach road, the intention being to ensure passengers had the shortest route to the 'railway' entrance, the family having to walk slightly further. Thus Droxford, Wickham and Privett were all as seen here. Whether by intention or design, each station building and also the signal box at each station, alternated on each side of the track.
Hampshire Record Office

A number of single men, not born locally, boarded in private houses. Five were at 'The Royal Oak', one at the 'Plough Inn' and another at 'The Falcon'. Married men had their families with them, such as Robert Whitfield 43, a ganger plate worker born in Ringwood. With him in Chiphall was his wife Annie 46, born in Devon, two daughters, and a one year old son born in Wickham. Two navvies boarded with them: William Cabbett 50, born in Northampton, and Henry Smith 40, born in Chichester.

A 'Railway Hut', close to Churchers Cottages, was occupied by Edwin Brening 32, a foreman born in Somerset with his wife Rose 30, born in Devon, his sister aged 15, and his children, Rose 8, Edith 5, both born in Devon, George 5 born in Kent, Mary 2 and Henry 4 months, both born in Devon. Four unmarried men boarded with them: William Bedford 54, a stoker born in Ireland and three

labourers, John Brown 41, born in Scotland, Thomas Smith 75 and George Back 17 both born in Dorset.

There was a similar hut in Brockbridge where William Piper 26, a 'horse hirer' born in Cornwall, lived with his wife Beatrice 22, born in Devon and their daughter Winifred 2, born in Padstow in Cornwall, and five boarders aged from 22 to 33, all single and navvies.

James Miles 38, an 'engine driver for Railway Contractor', his wife and six young children lived in Brockbridge but most railway workers lived further south in the parish, and in the village. Only two boarded in Droxford: Walter Freemantle 20, a carter, born in Droxford, and James Pratt 45, a foreman. Most of the railway workers were born in Hampshire and other southern counties, particularly Dorset, Somerset, Devon and Cornwall, perhaps because the contractors were from Plymouth[11].

Canon Benham, probably writing of West Meon, was very impressed in 1900 by the navvies who 'swarm in the streets of the quiet village, and it is a pleasure to have to write that the people like them and their ways so far:

" . . . There they were, as decent fellows as need be so far as I saw'. He described how two local men had taken over a large house and converted it into a restaurant and store with a bakehouse, where a good dinner of meat, vegetables and bread was supplied for 6d and a pint of 'wholesome beer' for 2d; 'A good many of them are total abstainers and there was a perfect army of beverages to suit them . . . There are carts which go a round of fifteen miles a day to the several centres of navvy labour to carry the bread and meat"[12].

Others in West Meon saw the navvies in a different light. According to the author of *West Meon, some chapters in its history*, there was a camp of huts there where the navvies lived:

"There were many drunken fights at the pubs particularly at the Hut and the Horseshoes at Woodlands, the two nearest to the camp . . . In the village the locals would not drink with the navvies. At the White Horse . . . a hut was built in the sunk garden next to the road for the navvies and the locals went indoors. Most Saturdays nights there was trouble. Sometimes the police were able to stop it, sometimes they turned a blind eye"[13].

In West Meon, families were threatened with eviction from tied cottages, such as those belonging to the Basing Park estate, if any of their men were navvies, while a number of illegitimate children were born[14]. The 1901 census for

Soberton appears to present a different situation: local navvies in Soberton lived at home, and incomers boarded with local families while there is no evidence of a camp, only two huts where boarders lived with a family.

In 1901, the 'Railway Hotel' opened at the entrance to the new Station Road, close to the intended station at Brockbridge, its licence having been transferred, as the navvies moved on, from 'The Three Horseshoes' at Woodlands, near Privett[15].

This was the end of the great age of railway construction, and of the railway navvies; men free of working long hours in factories, who were most often single and moved from job to job, and often ate fourteen or eighteen pounds of beef a week. When the Meon valley railway was built, two steam excavators and twenty men did the work that, a half century earlier, would have needed two hundred navvies[16].

The station buildings

The architect of the five stations and other buildings was Thomas Phillips Figgis (1858-1948), born in Dublin, who became an associate of the Royal Institute of Architects in 1889 and a fellow in 1900[17]. Having married Caroline M. Paton in Nottinghamshire in 1891, in the 1901 census, they lived at 10 Camden Hill Square in Kensington with two young sons, a cook and a housemaid.

The buildings at each station were of an identical design, and influenced by the Arts and Crafts Movement. Built of red brick in mock-Tudor style, with Portland Stone mullions and gables, they were described in 1903 as 'handsome and commodious'[18]. There were stained-glass windows in the doors and tiled interiors. Lavatories, on the platforms, were built in the style of Chinese pagodas[19]. The station was 'a large elegant building with a fine frontage. Two carefully shaped gables stand forward from a hipped roof'[20]. The five stations are said to be 'the most expensive stations per head-of-population served to be

11. TNA, RG 13/1090.
12. Stone, *Meon Valley Railway*, p. 34.
13. D:\SWC Meon Valley Portfolio R9D\construction 02.htm
14. D:\SWC Meon Valley Portfolio R9D\construction 02.htm
15. Stone, *Meon Valley Railway*, p. 22.
16. Coleman, *Railway Navvies*, pp. 199-205.
17. *The R.I.B.A. Kalendar*, 1939-40.
18. *The Railway Magazine*, 'Extension of the London and South-Western Railway', vol. 12 (January to July 1903), pp. 499-505
19. http://en.wikipedia.org/wiki/Meon_Valley_Railway
20. Binney, M. & Pearce, D., (ed), *Railway Architecture*, (London, 1979), p. 98.

Mr Yeates 'enjoying a pint in a Droxford hostelry'. Taken c1925, it was reported that Mr Yates had been involved in the construction of the railway, although it is not known in what capacity.

Ray Stone collection

built in the United Kingdom, and some of the finest rural stations of the late Victorian age[21].

In 1906 and 1908, Figgis's office was 28 St. Martin's Lane, Cannon Street [22]. By 1927, it was at 9 Old Square in Lincolns Inn, and he lived with his family at 15 Elm Road in Beckenham, south-east London[23]. 'An accomplished architect of some repute', he was architectural adviser to the Presbyterian Church of England[24].

Droxford Station was probably built in 1902, with the station building on the east side of the track. (The view on page 22 depicts the station surrounded by

scaffolding). In front was Station Road, the new road cut through the chalk to provide access from Brockbridge and the road crossing the Meon, and from Soberton village and Hambledon. On 21 March 1904 a photograph taken in Station Road, just north of the station building and forecourt, shows the 5th Isle of Wight 'Princess Beatrice's' Volunteer Brigade, Hampshire Regiment, who had arrived by train to march to their training camp. (see pages 42 and 43.) .Watching them was a young boy with a horse and farm cart. The road surface consisted of bare chalk, with bare chalk banks at the side of the road. There was trellis fencing and grass on the ground at the top of the bank separating the road from the railway track[25].

A double track ran through the station, with a 600 foot long platform on both sides, connected by a wooden bridge. The line became single track almost immediately north of the platforms but double track continued for a distance towards Fareham. Just south of the platforms, were points, with rail track leading to the sidings on the west side of the station. The movement of engines was controlled by a signal box on the west platform. According to the poster advertising the opening of the line (opposite) there was 'siding accommodation for Goods Traffic' at Mislingford, mainly to serve a local pumping station, and Farringdon, originally known as Faringdon. Each passenger station had also goods sidings, with an ornate goods shed built in corrugated iron, and hand-operated cranes for parcels and goods to be put on or taken off freight trains[26]. The original road to Soberton provided access to the sidings, with facilities for dealing with horses, livestock, carriages and carts[27].

Apart from the bridge on the north side and the gap through which the track passed southwards, the station was surrounded by chalk banks. By the south east boundary was a terrace of four new railway cottages, these adjoining the cottages which were there before the railway was built.

Completion

In November 1901, the LSWR applied for an extension of the time allowed for building the railway and other works authorised by the South Western (Meon

21. http://en.wikipedia.org/wiki/Meon_Valley_Railway
22. *The Architects & Surveyors Directory and Referendum*, 1906 and 1908.
23. *The R.I.B.A. Kalendar*, 1926-7. By 1933, they lived at 10 Stanley Avenue, Beckenham. He retired in 1940.
24. http://www.british-history.ac.uk/report.aspx?compid=46472: 'Poplar High Street: Public housing', *Survey of London*: volumes 43 and 44: Poplar, Blackwall and Isle of Dogs (1994), pp. 90-7.
25. HRO, 217M84/56/26.
26. http://en.wikipedia.org/wiki/Meon_Valley_Railway
27. Stone, *Meon Valley Railway*, p. 33.

Valley) Railway Act 1897[28]. The railway line, now due to open in March 1903 was further delayed by signalling works, bad weather and problems in building the line from Soberton southwards. The soil changed from chalk to the Reading Beds, clay containing stones, at Selworth Lane which was difficult to work: throughout the life of the line, the embankment would slip at Hooker Dene, and a low concrete wall had to be built at Mislingford to prevent clay flowing onto the track in wet weather[29].

The report of the Board of Trade's Inspecting Officer arrived at the Board of Trade on 6 April 1903: he reported that, at Droxford:

> ...Up trains in view of the rising gradient must be placed in sidings before shunting is commenced, & provision for this has been made. The frame [in the signal box] contains 24 levers of which 5 are spare . . . It will be necessary to fix lamps, and clocks at all the stations, before opening the new line for traffic, and the connections with signals & points will have to be made, and existing trap points removed . . .

Once the LSWR confirmed that the new railway was equipped for single line working, using the 'electric tablet system' installed at each station, he advised the Board of Trade to authorise the new railway for passenger traffic[30]. It opened on 1 June 1903.

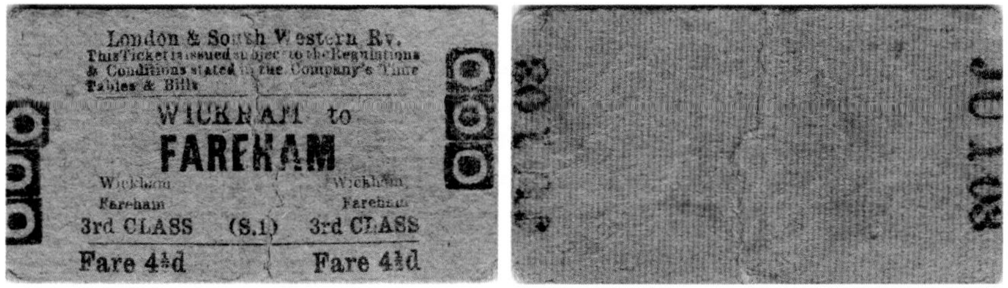

***Above -** Not from Droxford, unfortunately, but a potentially unique survivor in the form of the front and rear of the very first ticket ever issued from Wickham for travel on the Meon Valley Railway to Fareham, 1 June 1903.*
Ray Stone collection

28. *The London Gazette*, 22 November 1901, p. 7712.
29. Stone, *Meon Valley Railway*, p. 28.
30. Stone, *Meon Valley Railway*, pp. 111-8.

***Right -** Internal opening notices circulated with the London & South Western Railway.* *National Railway Museum*

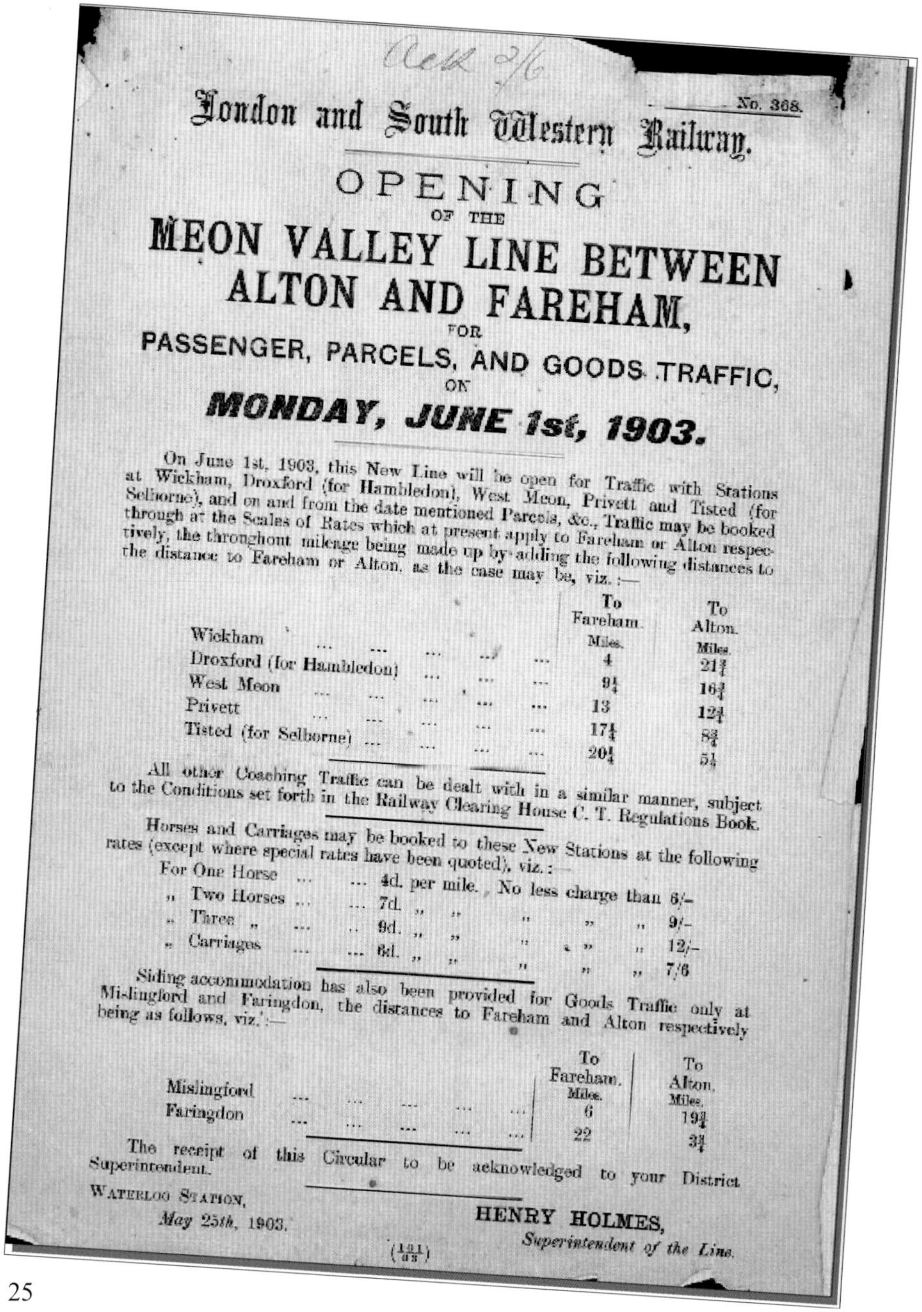

No. 368.

London and South Western Railway.

OPENING OF THE MEON VALLEY LINE BETWEEN ALTON AND FAREHAM, FOR PASSENGER, PARCELS, AND GOODS TRAFFIC, ON MONDAY, JUNE 1st, 1903.

On June 1st, 1903, this New Line will be open for Traffic with Stations at Wickham, Droxford (for Hambledon), West Meon, Privett and Tisted (for Selborne), and on and from the date mentioned Parcels, &c., Traffic may be booked through at the Scales of Rates which at present apply to Fareham or Alton respectively, the throughout mileage being made up by adding the following distances to the distance to Fareham or Alton, as the case may be, viz.:—

	To Fareham. Miles.	To Alton. Miles.
Wickham	4	21¾
Droxford (for Hambledon)	9¼	16¾
West Meon	13	12¼
Privett	17¼	8¾
Tisted (for Selborne)	20¼	5¼

All other Coaching Traffic can be dealt with in a similar manner, subject to the Conditions set forth in the Railway Clearing House C. T. Regulations Book.

Horses and Carriages may be booked to these New Stations at the following rates (except where special rates have been quoted), viz.:—

For One Horse	4d. per mile.	No less charge than 6/-
" Two Horses	7d. " "	" " " 9/-
" Three "	9d. " "	" " " 12/-
" Carriages	6d. " "	" " " 7/6

Siding accommodation has also been provided for Goods Traffic only at Mislingford and Faringdon, the distances to Fareham and Alton respectively being as follows, viz.:—

	To Fareham. Miles.	To Alton. Miles.
Mislingford	6	19¾
Faringdon	22	3¾

The receipt of this Circular to be acknowledged to your District Superintendent.

WATERLOO STATION,
May 25th, 1903.

HENRY HOLMES,
Superintendent of the Line.

Pristine Droxford with a train for Alton shortly to depart. Note the goods shed in the background. Although undated it is very likely the scene is within a few months of opening: an omission being the smoke troughs not yet fitted to the underside of the footbridge.   *Noodle Books collection.*

4
THE RAILWAY OPENS

There was no official opening ceremony when the Meon Valley Railway opened on Whit Monday, 1 June 1903. It was a Bank Holiday, and local people were allowed one free single journey to the next station[1]. On 3 July, children at Soberton School went by train on a day trip to Lee-on-the-Solent[2].

Page 25 shows the poster which announced its opening. 'Droxford (for Hambledon)' Station was 9¼ miles from Fareham and 16¾ miles from Alton. Horses and carriages could be booked to the new stations, the charges being:

One horse – 4d per mile, a minimum charge of 6s.

Two horses – 7d per mile, a minimum charge of 9s.

Three horses – 9d per mile, a minimum charge of 12s.

Carriages - 6d per mile, a minimum charge of 7s 6d.

There were eight to eleven services a day each way on the line, with trains having six or eight coaches. Each day, there were five through trains each way. Twice a day, a fast express train passed through between London and Gosport hauled by a Drummond T9 *Greyhound*. Through trains between Waterloo and Gosport were hauled by Adams *Jubilee* Class 0-4-2 locomotives. Local trains between Alton and Fareham used Adams *Radial* tank engines[3]. The locomotives and carriages were in the LSWR livery of sage green with a purple-brown edging, which created green panels, further lined in black and white. 'LSWR' was in gilt on the sides of the tender tank.

Six local passenger trains ran each way from Monday to Saturday, with an additional late train on Saturday evenings, and two trains each way on a Sunday. On Saturdays, the last train left Gosport at 9.40 p.m. At Fareham, it connected

with the 9.15 p.m. from Portsmouth, and stopped at all stations before terminating at West Meon, and beginning its return journey, giving villagers an opportunity to enjoy early evening activities in Gosport and Fareham[4].

On Sundays in the summer, special excursion trains took passengers to the coast from inland towns such as Aldershot, Woking and Ascot[5]. By the summer of 1912, there were cheap week-end tickets from Friday to Sunday from Waterloo, Vauxhall, Queens Road, Hammersmith, Shepherds Bush, Kennington, West Brompton, Chelsea and Fulham, Battersea, Clapham, Clapham Junction and Wimbledon to stations on the line, and to Bentworth and Lasham, Medstead and Bursledon. A first class ticket to Droxford Station cost 14s 0d, a second class ticket 8s 9d and a third class ticket was 7s 0d. Once there, it was a short walk to eat, drink and relax at the Railway Hotel[6].

The Station Master

Each station had its own station master, three signalmen, porters and office staff[7].

Commercial postcard.

1. Stone, R.A., *The Meon Valley Railway*, (Southampton, 1983), p. 36.
2. Information from Ann Pendred, the outing being recorded in the school's logbook held at Hampshire Record Office.
3. http://en.wikipedia.org/wiki/Meon_Valley_Railway
4. D:\SWC Meon Valley Portfolio R9D\passwork02.htm
5. Stone, *Meon Valley Railway*, p. 36.
6. Stone, *Meon Valley Railway*, p. 124.
7. Stone, *Meon Valley Railway*, p. 33.

The station master and his family lived in a house, which was an integral part of the station building, being on the left hand side at Droxford Station. The booking hall, giving access to the platform, was in the middle, with the ticket office on the right hand side. A fitted wooden counter ran the full width of the ticket office, with built in cupboards and drawers below, those below the booking hatch window having narrow partitions to hold tickets. The waiting area was in the booking hall, and the ladies' waiting room, with a fire and seats, to the left of the booking hall.

No money was wasted on staffing by the railway company: Droxford's first station master, Frank Wills, began work there on 1 June 1903, the day the rail service began. Born in Fordingbridge, his father was a railway guard. The railways were almost a closed shop, a practice which continued until 1940: applicants related to a railway worker might be considered, but others from totally outside the 'railway family' were rejected[8].

Aged fifteen, Frank began with the London & South Western Railway in October 1886 as a junior clerk at Dorchester Station earning 10s a week, moving to Broadstone in Canford Magna in October 1889 where, in the 1891 census, he was a railway booking clerk. Aged 20, he lived with his wife Charlotte Ada 21 and their son Reginald Frank 3 months old[9]. Charlotte Ada died in late 1896[10].

In 1893, he earned £1. 3s a week. He transferred to Botley Station in October 1894 and became one of the salaried staff, earning £70 a year and, in 1901, remained a railway booking clerk, now married to Lydia 29. Besides Reginald, aged 10, he had 3 more children: Gladys Ada 4, William Henry 2 and Albert Willoughby 9 months, all born in Botley[11].

He applied for the position of station master at Droxford, with a salary of £80 a year and a free house, which rose to £90 a year in January 1906[12]. In the 1911 census, Frank and Lydia lived in the Station House with his widowed mother

and their five children: Gladys Ada 14, William Henry 12, Albert Willoughby 10, Edwin John 8, all born in Botley, and Ida Ellen 6, born in Droxford. It was a full house with eight occupants: besides the kitchen and any bathroom, there were four other rooms[13]. A month before the census, Frank Wills' eldest son, Reginald Frank, lived there as well.

Frank Wills had recommended Reginald for employment with the LSWR but lied about his son's age: LSWR's records have his date of birth as 29 December 1889, a year earlier than his actual birth. Staff had to be fifteen years old before they began work with the company but Reginald, aged fourteen and a half, probably left school in July 1904. He immediately began work with his father at Droxford Station as an office lad at 8s a week, rising to 10s in October 1905, 12s in February 1907, 13s in February 1908 and 14s in March 1910. The following month, Reginald became an office porter at 16s a week and, in March 1911, transferred to Portsmouth Station as a parcels clerk. Moving to Fratton in 1913, he was conscripted in 1917, returning to duty in 1919[14].

For Frank Wills and his four successors, being at Droxford Station was a step towards becoming station master at a larger station with a bigger salary. In November 1912, he moved to Ropley Station with a salary of £100 a year and, in 1919, to Millbrook Station where he earned £120 a year[15].

He was succeeded in 1912 by William Mitchell who lived alone in the Station House, having previously been at Privett[16]. Mitchell, who began with the LSWR in 1887, received £90 a year and a free house until he transferred to Worplesdon in March 1917, and was replaced by Arthur Phillips and his family [17].

Arthur Phillips began with the company in 1894, aged fifteen and employed at Petersfield Station as a junior porter earning 7s a week He became a parcel porter in 1897, and was paid 13s a week. In March 1898, he became an office porter at Elsted earning 15s a week, and moved to Alton earning 18s a week. In

8. Wolmar, Christian, *Fire and Steam*, (London, 2007), p. 256.
9. TNA, GRO RG12/1637/21.
10. TNA, GRO Death indexes.
11. TNA, GRO RG13/1065/19.
12. TNA, RAIL 411/494: information about Frank Will's career with the LSWR.
13. http://www.1911census.co.uk/search/tnaform.aspx
14. TNA, RAIL 411/494, RAIL 411/511.
15. TNA, RAIL/411/494.
16. HRO, H/CL9/4/299.
17. TNA, RAIL/411/498.

February 1900 he earned £1 a week, and, a year later, transferred to Kingston where he was promoted to a 'weekly paid clerk' at £1. 2s 6d a week. This rose to £1. 5s the following year, and £1. 7s 6d in April 1903.

In July 1905, he was placed on the salary staff earning £85 a year, rising to £100 in January 1914. Arriving at Droxford in March 1917, he earned £85 a year with 'a free house etc' and, from January 1919, £90 a year with a free house. His salary became £200 a year in August 1919, with a bonus of £25 (Class 5), presumably paying rent for his accommodation. In February 1920, Phillips transferred to Overton Station, a Class 4 position with a salary beginning at £210 a year plus a bonus[18].

His successor, Ernest Owen Cobley, began as a signal lad at Pirbright Station in 1888, earning 6s a week. In 1891, he became an office porter at Hook earning 11s a week before moving to Midhurst in 1892. His pay regularly increased until he was appointed to the salaried staff in November 1900 at £70 a year, having transferred to Farnborough Station two months earlier. In 1916 he earned £110 a year but, in 1920, became Station Master (Class 5) at Droxford at £90 a year, with a free house etc. and a bonus of £25 a year. Cobley moved to Hurstbourne Station (Class 4) in August 1924, beginning at £230 a year with an annual bonus. Arthur Powell, who joined the company in 1898, succeeded Cobley in August 1924, with a salary of £200 a year and remained there in 1927, living in the Station House with his family[19].

In 1914, a manual was published for station staff and signalmen working for the London and Midland railway, but its authors wrote that most of it applied to all railway companies. They wrote that, in a small station, the station master kept all under his direct supervision, it being essential that he be

> ...smart, energetic, and possessed of a fair amount of business acumen. His relationship both with the public and with his staff will require the exercise of tact and consideration. He must see that the public are treated in a courteous manner and that efforts are promptly made to satisfy their requirements . . . all questions raised by his staff have to be enquired into with fairness and impartiality. Complaints of officialdom and petty tyranny, the two greatest incentives to labour unrest, must be especially guarded against.

18. TNA, RAIL/411/500
19. TNA, RAIL/411/498.

An early snapshot of an unidentified person whose photograph was taken in the goods yard at Droxford. Although undated the background fortunately includes the west side of the goods shed which is not seen in any other photographs.
Ray Stone Collection

The first essential was to keep the station and its precincts clean and tidy, with up-to-date posters and excursion bills. The station was to be inspected daily to ensure waiting rooms, offices, platforms and lavatories were 'in proper condition'. All staff wore uniforms, being expected to look smart. For safety reasons, platform edges were to be kept whitened, and a watchful eye kept on fire buckets to ensure they were 'kept full of clean water, except during frosty weather, when they should be emptied to prevent the formation of ice and the consequent bursting of the buckets'.

He should be on the platform when trains arrived, and the porters ready, the guard and the staff using 'prompt efforts' to take out and put in parcels, and 'to hasten passengers to their seats, the stationmaster giving the "Ready" signal to the guard as punctually as possible'.

He must 'take a keen interest in the working of trains through his station', but be careful not to destroy initiative on the part of the signalman. He had to be able to take charge of a signal-box if no relief staff were available, check horses for wounds or injuries before a horse-box was loaded, and be responsible for and supervise a certain stretch of line on either side of his station, and all traffic operation within his jurisdiction.

Without modern weather forecasting, fog and snow could develop without warning, and the stationmaster was to take charge ensuring 'fogmen', drawn from the ranks of the platelayers or traffic and goods staff if there were insufficient platelayers, were in position, each with 36 detonators, a hand lamp, and red and green flags to stop an approaching train if necessary. This was particularly important on the Meon Valley line which was mainly single track.

The station master, responsible to the district superintendent, was to report anything outside the usual routine, informing him of any special events locally such as fairs, shows and horse-racing which could enable them to run excursion trains, and to promote the railway company. His duties were summarised at the end of the manual:

He should be both courteous with the public and tactful with the staff. The public will forego many complaints, and perhaps claims, if they have a civil and obliging stationmaster. Moreover, his bearing will have an effect on the company's receipts for often is he called upon to canvass for political and race meetings, etc., and be the means of securing traffic against strong competition.

Thus, the stationmaster's duties are many and varied. Innumerable, indeed, are the circumstances under which a stationmaster has to act with quick judgement, sound discretion and courtesy, and the various qualities required for the due discharge of all these functions are the systematic arrangement of station duties, the effective direction of staff and familiarity with all branches of railway operation[20].

The Station House was continuously occupied but it is not known whether later station masters lived there, as the LSWR's staff records end in 1923 when it became part of Southern Railway. At some stage, the station master at Wickham became responsible for Droxford Station while Catherine Walder was the only person over the age of twenty-one in the house from 1933 to 1935.

Harold William Foster, born in 1899, who lived at the Station House in 1936-7, was the son of the station master at Wickham Station. Recommended by his father, he joined the railway company in 1914 as an office lad at Wickham. In 1915, he transferred to West Meon before working at Fareham as a parcels porter. Conscripted in March 1917 to join the army, no more is known of his career[21].

Occupants of the Station House from 1906 to 1939, taken from the electoral registers[22].

Year	Occupants eligible to vote
1906-7	Frank Wills
1911 census	*Frank Wills and family*
1914	William Mitchell
1918-20	Arthur & Elizabeth Charlotte Phillips
1920-4	Ernest Owen & Mabel Florence Cobley
1925-7	Arthur & Ethel Mary Powell
1928-32	Percy Henry & Ellen Adams
1933-5	Catherine Emily Walder
1936-7	Harold William & Catherine Emily Foster
1938-9	Charles Percy & Sarah Edith Jolly

The Booking Office

As now, there was a wide range of tickets: single and return first class, second

20. Jenkinson, John A., Lamb, David R. & Travis, Charles, *Railway Operation: The Passenger Station and Signalling*, (London, 1914), pp. 145-53, 161-73.
21. TNA, RAIL 411/513.
22. HRO, H/CL9/4/295-328.

The original station clock from Droxford. Notwithstanding that the face has been repainted 'B.R.(S)' to indicate 'British Railways - Southern', it is a remarkable survivor. It now belongs in a private collection.

Simon Turner

23. Jenkinson, *Railway Operation,* pp. 10-32.

class and third class tickets, but also excursion, market day, workmen's, tourists and other cheap tickets. Policemen, soldiers, sailors and others had vouchers for reduced fares and, on showing a warrant, free fares were available to Post Office staff. When on duty, Post Office and Postal Telegraph engineers, soldiers and sailors had free fares if a warrant was produced. Commercial travellers' weekend tickets allowed them to go home and return for the cost of a single ticket.

There were bicycle and dog tickets, with local tickets for passengers travelling just on that railway company's trains, with foreign tickets for those using other companies' trains. Once a train departed, tickets issued for that train were recorded in a Ticket Book, with local tickets in their geographical order, and in the Classification Book which recorded tickets sold that day, with foreign tickets recorded separately. Each month, a passenger classification summary was sent to the Audit Office, with cancelled and cut portions of tickets pasted in the proper order on a sheet of paper and sent in a special envelope.

Guidelines issued to new booking clerks concluded:

> Keep your head and don't give too much change.
> Remember to cut adult tickets when issued to children, and carefully preserve the snips; also cut privilege tickets when issued in favour of females.
> Alter your dating press each night after departure of the last train.
> Be courteous to enquirers and always push your own route[23].

Luggage

Few people had their own cars, and first class passengers were allowed to take with them, as personal luggage, up to 150 lbs, second class, where provided, up to 120 lbs and third class 100 lbs. Luggage, bearing a special green label with the words 'Luggage in Advance' plainly written and stating the destination station, could be sent in advance.

'Excursionists' could only carry 'small handbags, luncheon baskets, or other small articles intended for the passenger's use during the day, although those with excursion tickets covering periods of more than one day could take up to 60 lbs at their own risk.

Commercial travellers and music hall artists, etc., were allowed 3 hundred weight if travelling first-class and 1½ hundred weight third-class. For groups of artistes or theatrical companies, trucks were provided for the free conveyance of

This page - Two early views of the J E Smith coal merchant's office and a Vulcan (30cwt?), lorry, the latter dating from some time after 1916 although more likely to have been in the 1920s. The identities of the men seen are not known, while the same dog may be seen in both images - uncharacteristically perhaps still with white fur bearing in mind the ownership! Whilst it was the practice for various merchants to sometimes own their own railway wagons, these were invariably labelled towards the larger stations from where the firm operated. It was unlikely Droxford would have appeared on the side of any wagons.

Ray Stone collection

Bottom - A chance find in the form of one of a handful of pages from the Droxford coal delivery book, circa 1906. Whether this was a railway or merchant's document is not completely clear, possibly the latter, for the simple reason the initials 'L&SWR' might otherwise be expected to be shown. Slightly difficult to read perhaps, but the information contained across the page indicates the date the coal was received, the consignee, the truck number and weight of coal, plus the date of advice (presumably the date the station were advised the truck was on the way) and in the penultimate column, the date of delivery. The occasional entry under the 'Charges' column may refer to a demurrage (delay unloading) payment made. *Denis Tillman collection*

scenery, etc., as follows, the trucks going by the same train as the passengers:

21 to 33 adult passengers 1 truck (21 feet) free
34 to 66   "   "   2 trucks   "   "
67 to 100 "   "   3   "   "   "

One extra truck was allowed for every additional 33 passengers, and 3d per truck per mile for all luggage carried in excess of the free allowance.

Railway companies were compelled to carry passengers' luggage, and certain perishable goods by Act of Parliament. These were milk, fresh butter, fresh cheese, cream, eggs, fish, hothouse fruit and vegetables, dead game, dead rabbits, dead poultry, and fresh meat. Livestock could be carried by passenger train, but the company's liability under the Regulation of Railways Act 1854 was limited to horses, neat cattle, asses or mules, sheep, pigs, dogs, deer, goats, rabbits or other small quadrupeds, and poultry or other birds[24].

24. Jenkinson, *Railway Operation*, pp. 24, 36-9, 47-8, 78-9.

Station Hotel Droxford

The Railway Hotel, Droxford; later known as the 'Station Hotel' until c1929/1930 - see page 50. . Usually described as being in Droxford, it and Droxford. Station were in Brockbridge, a small community just in the parish of Soberton. Station Road is seen on the right: a new road provided by the railway as the route of the old road was buried under the new railway. To the left the road heads towards Hambledon, whilst behind it drops down under the railway. The station was a few yards along Station Road. Opened in 1901, the alcohol licence had been transferred from 'The Three Horseshoes' near Privett. Droxford and Privett were the only stations to boast such a nearby hotel facility although there would already have been hotels in Wickham and existing public house accommodation available near the other stations.

Kevin Robertson collection

Strawberry Traffic in South Hampshire

Strawberry traffic being loaded at nearby Wickham in 1908. No images of similar traffic which took place at Droxford have been located. Apart from railway staff and the grower on his horse, the presence of young boys will be noted. Boys were employed as they were able to reach easily under the seats of passenger carriages, the space being used to carry the fruit in the peak season.

Wickham parish Council, Stan Woodford collection.

The number of men employed demonstrated the volume of soft fruit from south Hampshire. This is Swanwick which, together with Botley, represented the principal areas where fruit was loaded during the season. As well as obvious railway staff, there were a number of casual workers.

Tony Williams collection / Alan A Jackson collection, and Lens of Sutton collection.

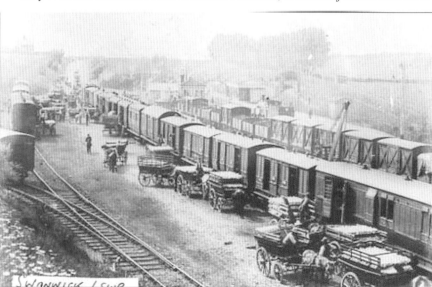

It is unfortunate but views of the railway cottages at Droxford are conspicuous by their absence. In this latter day scene looking north towards the station, the end wall of the railway cottages may be seen at the top of the embankment on the left. In the foreground the grindstone was used by the permanent way men to sharpen their tools: one man slowly pouring water on to the top whilst another turned the wheel.

Ray Stone collection

5
BEYOND THE STATION

Four railway cottages were built on the high ground to the west of the station, overlooking the goods yard, with two rooms downstairs including a kitchen and two upstairs.

Apart from those who owned or rented their own properties and were allowed to vote in local elections, women did not yet have the vote. Electoral registers for 1906 list six men at Brockbridge: Frank Wills, James Varndell and William Sheppard who lived in the nearby cottages, Harry Bright, a signal man, Henry William Rackett, a porter, and George Laishley, perhaps an incorrect spelling for Harry Lashly at the Station Hotel[1]. The following year, the register lists seven men: Frank Wills, William Sheppard, Harry Bright and Henry William Rackett as well as Henry Stanley Dykes, George Beer and Harry Trivett[2].

In the 1911 census, taken on the night of 2 April, the four families in the cottages were those of George Franklin, Frank Vine, Harry Bright and Albert McRill. While Franklin and Vine called them Station Cottages, Bright and McRill gave them as Railway Cottages. George Franklin 27, a plate layer born in Wickham, lived with his wife Ellen Mary 26, their daughter Evelyn 16 months old, and Arthur Harry White 24, a coal carter, who boarded with them

Frank Vine had been employed in building the railway, earning 6d a day. In the 1901 census, aged 21 and born in Southampton, he lived in Ropley with his wife Rose, also 21, and her family, employed as a 'tunnel miner'[4] 'Navvy'. Ten years later, he had been married to his second wife Kate, aged 40, for less than a year and had two sons, Ernest Edwin 9 and William 5, both born in Ropley. Mabel Marriner 17, a dairymaid, lived with them. His daily duties included walking the line between Droxford and Wickham Stations to report any dangerous subsidence. In World War Two, he served with the Home Guard[5]. In 1918, all men over 21 and all women over the age of 30 became able to vote and, in 1927, Frank Vine's son Edward Frank was old enough to vote.

Harry Bennett Bright aged 46, a railway signal man, lived with his wife Agnes 41, their son Harry George 15 and Harry's widowed mother Emma aged 86. In July 1911, he recommended his son Harry George Bright for employment in the LSWR. He became an office lad at West Meon Station, moving to Privett the following year, to Wickham in 1914 and to Brockenhurst in 1916 as an office porter[6]. Agnes Bright remained in her cottage for a year or so after her husband's death in 1926-7.

Years	1 or 2 Railway Cottages	1 or 2 Railway Cottages	3 Railway Cottages	4 Railway Cottages
1914-1926	George Franklin	Frank Vine	Harry Bright	Albert McRill
1927-1928	George Franklin	Frank Vine	Agnes Bright	Alfred South
No register for 1929-30				
1930-1937	George Franklin	Frank Vine	Reginald Young	Richard Carter
1938-1939	George Franklin	Frank Vine	Daniel Williams	Richard Carter

1. HRO, H/CL9/4/295.
2. HRO, H/CL9/4/296.
3. HRO, H/CL9/4/299-328.
4. TNA, RG13/1096/26.
5. Ward, Kenneth, *Droxford in the Meon Valley*, (Havant), p.7.
6. TNA, RAIL 411/512.

Heads of household of the Railway Cottages at Droxford Station taken from the electoral registers 1914-1939. The registers do not show which of the two families, the Franklins or the Vines, lived at 1 and 2 Railway Cottages[3].

Reginald and Louisa Young succeeded her, with Charles Percy Jolly lodging with them for over a year from 1935. Jolly and his wife lived in the Station House just before the Second World War. The Youngs were followed by Daniel Leslie and Violet Evelyn Williams in 1938.

Albert McRill was born in 1882 in Sholing, Southampton, the son of a 'checker on the railway' although LSWR's records have him born in 1885[7]. He began as a goods porter at Scholing in 1903, transferring to Bitterne in 1904 as a porter, before coming to Droxford on 1 April 1909. On 18 April he became a porter and relief signal man commencing at 18s a week. In the 1911 census, aged 26, he lived with his wife Eliza 23, also born in Scholing and Winifred 1, born in Soberton. On New Years Day 1920, he became a porter and signal man at £3 a week which gradually rose to £3. 10s a year later and then gradually reduced until he was paid £2. 9s a week in July 1923, because of the withdrawal of bonuses paid to allow for post-war inflation[8]. At 4 Railway Cottages, Alfred and Tryphena Rose South moved in during 1927 but, by late 1930, Richard and Kate Jane Carter lived there.

This page - *An undated (1920s?) view of the Hambledon Hunt's Meet at Droxford Station. Such meetings could take place as often as twice a week with the dates announced in advance in local newspapers.*

Opposite page - *Probably the same occasion. Soberton and Newtown Local History Society.*
Commercial postcards

7. TNA, RG 13/1063/43.
8. TNA, RAIL 411/510.

New villas

Mr F.J. Minchin, the absent lord of the manor and owner of Bushey Farm, would benefit through the sale of land and the building of new villas in Station Road, just south of the station, for an upper middle class community able to live less expensively in the country and to travel easily to London, using the connection at Alton. One villa had ten rooms, and the rest six to eight rooms, besides a kitchen. In 1907, nine new villas were occupied, six of which had women as the householder and, in 1915, nineteen villas, including twelve with a woman as the householder[9]. Locally, they were known as 'the widows' villas'[10]. (See photograph on page 41.)

In the 1911 census, there were twelve households in residence, Lt. Col. Fletcher being absent. Nearly every house had at least one servant living in. Five were headed by a single or widowed woman, all with private means. Of the remaining seven male householders, Frederick Fanstone 40, Richard Gason 39 and Henry Stanley Parsons 58 had private means. Three were retired, namely George Elphick, a former architect, Charles Merrington, a former Indian civil servant and Vice-Admiral Paget. Only one householder worked: the local cab-proprietor Charles Lunn 68, at Hambledon House.

In *Kelly's Directory* in 1915, the householders were Miss Allen (High Croft), Miss Fergie, Miss Hamilton, Miss Jackson, Miss Peters, Miss Roberts, Mrs Beaty-Pownall, Mrs Burkitt, Mrs Elkington, Mrs Lysart-Griffin, Mrs Robinson, Mrs Ross-Johnson, Capt. Henry Montague Doughty, R.N., George Harold Elphick (Aldersyde), Lt. Col. Henry Arthur Fletcher, C.V.O., Huie H. Greville, Charles Merrington, and Vice-Admiral Arthur Cecil Henry Paget.

For Lt. Col. Fletcher, already living there in 1907, it was a second home. Serving in the Bengal Cavalry from 1860-89, he was on the north-west frontier of India in 1863-4 and in the Egyptian Campaign in 1882. He married in 1881, but had no children. From 1900, he was clerk of the Cheque and Adjutant to the monarch's Body Guard of the Honourable Corps of Gentlemen-at Arms, and in the War Office from 1909. Based at St. James's Palace, his main home was at 17 Victoria Square, Westminster, until 1917, and he belonged to the Garrick and United Services Clubs. He died in 1921[11].

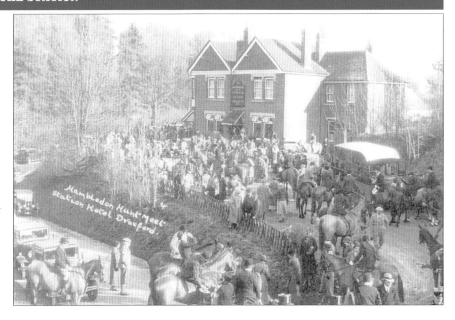

Local trade

The LSWR was profitable, normally paying out 5½ per cent or more in dividends after 1871 and, although it primarily carried passengers, nearly 40 per cent of its revenues in 1908 came from its steamships, docks and freight, the first decade of the 1900s having seen a rapid growth in goods traffic on the railways. The Company had expansive plans, as seen in the Meon Valley Railway, and was continually widening track and making improvements but its management was slow to identify change or opportunities. Provision had been made for a mainline railway, but the vision was not promoted and the timetable (see Appendix 3) was inconvenient for early or late passenger travel to and from London. With the Boer War, military traffic had increased, and there was a threatening situation in mainland Europe which would lead to World War One, but the Company made little effort to persuade the War Office to use the line. The LSWR appointed a new general manager in 1912, Herbert Walker, a shrewd man who brought about major change, such as the electrification of

9. *Kelly's Directory of Hampshire, Wiltshire, Dorset and the Channel Islands*, 1907; *Kelly's Directory of Hampshire and the Isle of Wight*, 1915.
10. Information from Tony Williams.
11. *Who's Who*.

High Street Soberton, probably between 1905 and 1910. The two nearest shops were not built until a few years into the 20th century, whereas the furthest shop - that with a differing pitch to the roof - came earlier. In a 1907 Kelly's trade directory covering the area, Miss Mary G Anderson is recorded as keeping the post office. Prior to Miss Anderson, it was been run by someone with the surname Hoad and, in 1911, by Miss Helen Slade. At the time of the photograph the middle shop appears empty. The land on which these were built was purchased from the Lord of the Manor for £60 by Mr Melhuish of Yew Tree Farm in 1899.

Soberton and Newtown Local History Society

Soberton Community.

Top left - *The new villas in Station Road.*

Top right - *Soberton school.*

Bottom right - *Charabanc trip setting out from 'The Plough' in Forester Road, Soberton. Unfortunately there are no details of the likely destination. The image also indicated that already, local people were less dependent upon the railway for travel.*
Soberton and Newtown Local History Society

This page and opposite - Military manoeuvres at Droxford, 1904. Whether these were recorded on the same occasion is uncertain. In the view on the right the route of the new Station Road through the hillside is apparent, the chalk having yet to attract growth on the cutting's side. Notice also the condition of the road surface. It was not until a few years later that a programme of metalled roads was embarked upon throughout Hampshire and, even then, routes such as this may not have been priorities.

The number of troops arriving at Droxford by train was due to an increase in territorial army reservists, many having served in the Boar War, and the beginnings of a fear of German militarism.

suburban lines, but kept a sharp eye on the finances and what was profitable for the Company[12].

Local landowners supported the construction of the railway, but the age of the car was beginning and they would be the first to buy them, for they enabled independent travel. The doctor was said to be the first in Soberton to have a car[13]. Most local people were yet to buy one, but could use the train service to reach nearby towns, London and the south coast. However, it was after World War One before passengers using Droxford Station could reach Fareham before 9.00 a.m. In May 1918, the first train to Fareham left at 9.37 a.m. but, soon after, Bert Lashley of Droxford attended Price's School in Fareham, travelling there on the 8.00 a.m. train down, and returning on the service leaving at 4.30 p.m[14]. The main source of income for the railway came from transporting agricultural goods. It transformed life for the rural community. At every station, churns of milk were brought by horse and cart, and transferred to milk vans attached to passenger trains to be transported to Portsea Island Co-operative Dairy. Livestock was carried to and from the markets at Alton and Fareham[15]. On market days, special trains had both passenger carriages and cars for animals, enabling farmers to travel with their livestock. Each day, there was one north-bound and one south-bound goods train, wagons and trucks being shunted at the goods yard by the locomotive, which uncoupled at each station and marshalled the wagons and trucks, there being no shunting engines on the line[16].

The southern part of the line ran through an area of market gardening. In the 1901 census, there were twenty-nine market gardeners in Soberton, mainly in Hundred Acres in the south of the parish: their produce was sent to market in railway box vans. Known as the Strawberry Line, in the summer, 'strawberry specials', complete trainloads of locally grown strawberries, left the goods yards at Wickham and Mislingford.

Eventually, every station on the line had at least one coal merchant[17].

12. Simmons, J. & Biddle, N., (eds), *The Oxford Companion to British Railway History*, (Oxford 1997, 1999 ed.), p. 286, p.555.
13. Ann Pendred.
14. D:\SWC Meon Valley Portfolio R9D\password02.htm
15. Stone, *Meon Valley Railway*, p. 42.
16. http://en.wikipedia.org/wiki/Meon_Valley_Railway

According to Denis Tillman, the Colliery Supply Company had coal staithes at Droxford Station in 1907[18]. No coal merchants were advertised there in *Kelly's Directory* for 1907 and 1911, although Isaac W. Knight was a coal merchant in Droxford in 1911[19]. In 1915 and 1923, Read and Sons were in the station yard[20]. J.E. Smith (Portsmouth) Ltd., coal dealers, were at the station from at least 1927 through to the 1950s. Directories ceased during the Second World War but, in 1939, Samuel Courage was a coal and coke dealer in Soberton[21].

Before 1914, most goods sold in local shops came by train, including fish, and beer was delivered to the Station Hotel from Courage's Brewery at Alton[22]. Originally called the 'Railway Hotel', there was no mention of the Station Hotel in *Kelly's Directory* for 1907 but, in the directory for 1911, Harry Lashley ran the Station Hotel, and remained there until 1926-7. While he was there, it was listed in the electoral register as the 'Railway Hotel'[23]. Goods for Droxford were taken by horse and cart along

Mill Lane and through the ford in the mill stream, a practice which continued for many years[24].

There was still a place for the local carrier: Alfred Couzens did the return journey from Droxford to Southampton on Mondays, Portsmouth on Thursdays, passing through Soberton, and Winchester on Saturdays. In 1911 and 1915, Charles Lunn of Hambleton Cottage, in Station Road, was a 'cab proprietor'. Theodore Merrington and Frederick Bellingham were cycle agents in Droxford, but people still used horses for agriculture and local haulage; Arthur George Withers of Droxford was a harness maker[25].

Above - Hampshire Record Office 217M84/56/26.

17. Stone, *Meon Valley Railway*, p. 42.
18. Tillman, Denis, *The Meon Valley Revisited*, (Bishop's Waltham, 2003), p. 22.
19. *Kelly's Directory*, 1911.
20. *Kelly's Directory*, 1915, 1923.
21. *Kelly's Directory*, 1927, 1939.
22. Tillman, *Meon Valley*, p. 22. Ann Pendred was told that fish arrived by train for local parishes.
23. *Kelly's Directory*, 1911; *Kelly's Directory of Hampshire, Wiltshire, Dorset and the Channel Islands* 1923, part 1; HRO H/CL9/4/316.
24. HRO, 2/7M84/6.
25. *Kelly's Directory*, 1911.

Left - The Square looking up the hill south towards Wickham.

Bottom left - In this view, the photographer has turned around and is looking north towards Corhampton, Warnford and West Meon.

Scenes around Droxford

Above - Droxford Church.

Commercial cards / Tony Williams collection.

Right - A hand tinted commercial card looking down the hill towards The Square from the north, with the White Horse Inn on the right. None of the images on these pages are dated nor provide any information as to sender / addressee on the reverse.
Tony Williams collection.

Bottom left and right - A final image from the area. Brockbridge cottage is literally yards from the railway - the photographer having the railway bridge immediately north of the station at his back. The road on which the pedestrians are standing is now designated the B2150 from Droxford to Hambledon, one half of Mill lane also seen to the left with the other half just out of camera to the right. Beyond the corner the road leads up to the present day A32. Two almost identical images of the location have been found, the only difference being the pedestrians / horse visible. One is postmarked 15 December 1905 having been sent from Droxford to Mrs G Short of Fratton Road, Portsmouth. The message on the reverse was simple, "Many happy returns of the day, Alf and Nell", and "Write soon".

Tony Williams / Soberton and Newtown Local History Society collections.

Droxford through the years. Both images are viewed looking through the station - coincidentally, and purely for logistical reasons so far as the siting of the stations was concerned. Wickham was the only one of the five stations on the Meon Valley line not built on a curve.

In the top view, probably taken soon after opening, the track ballast is spread above the level of the sleepers - similar to that seen on page 26. This may simply be that fresh stone had been added and had yet to be spread. (The practice of covering the sleepers in the belief that it gave a more secure formation had fallen out of favour by this time, not least as with the sleepers covered it was difficult to detect deterioration.) Another reason why ballast was sometime used to cover sleepers was when a horse might be used to shunt wagons, unlikely at Droxford, although it cannot be ruled out for the simple expedience of perhaps shifting a wagon of coal a few feet for unloading.

The lower view records the scene a few years later, possibly in the early days of the Southern Railway, post 1923. The signal box nameboard had changed whilst shrubs and topiary flourish. For the present the wooden footbridge remains. Its subsequent removal was probably simply one of age, 20+ years, the limited traffic handled meaning a replacement was simply not warranted. Although unconfirmed, it is possible the goods sheds on the line were taken down around the same time. Whilst an inconvenience, goods traffic (except at Wickham) did not seem to warrant their retention, a saving of rates paid to the local council is likely to have been the principal consideration. Denis Tillman collection.

Below - *Southern Railway luggage label.*

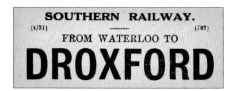

6
THE FIRST WORLD WAR AND BEYOND

When war was declared against Germany in August 1914, the line was used to carry troops to the docks, to cross to France. The government took control of the railways, forming a committee of eleven general managers of major railway companies with the president of the Board of Trade as chairman, but the driving force was Herbert Walker, general manager of the LSWR.

The British Expeditionary Force left from Southampton, the LSWR ensuring that, apart from the cancellation of some special holiday trains, the normal timetable continued. By the end of August, 118,000 men, 37,650 horses, 314 large guns, 1,800 bicycles and thousands of tons of baggage had arrived by rail: every train was on time or early, arriving at Southampton every twelve minutes for sixteen hours a day. By the end of the war, the LSWR had carried 20 million soldiers, an average of 13,000 a day[1].

Civilian passenger services were reduced and some were cut out. Railway staff and locomotives were sent to mainland Europe. In 1915, through fast services between Waterloo and Gosport were withdrawn from the line and never fully restored.

As the war continued, people had more money because of higher wages, but little to spend it on because of shortages, and seaside holidays became popular again although the government tried unsuccessfully to discourage train travel: from December 1916, they restricted luggage, which often comprised a trunk or several cases, to 100 lbs for each passenger. In early 1917, to discourage unnecessary passenger travel, fares were increased by 50 per cent, holiday trains no longer ran and new timetables were introduced with slower trains[2].

Local recruits and, from 1916, conscripts would have left from Droxford Station, probably seen off by families. Some did not return. Fourteen men who died are recorded on the memorial in Droxford Church, including Captain Alick Gregory Martin MC, of Princess Patricia's Canadian Light Infantry (Eastern

Ontario Division), who died in March 1918. Fifteen are remembered at Soberton, including all four sons of John and Mary Rachel Twynam of Soberton House, and others on the lych gate at Holy Trinity Church in Newtown.

Early in 1915, Vice Admiral Frederick Charles Doveton Sturdee (1859-1925), of Meon Lea in Droxford, and his wife were photographed on the platform at Droxford. Local residents awaited their train and greeted them on the platform, including Mrs. Nellie Reeves, a Droxford shopkeeper who was the local press agent. Mrs Sturdee received a large bouquet of flowers[3]. Appointed Chief of the War Staff in 1914 and Commandeer-in-Chief of the Atlantic and South Pacific Stations in 1914-5, the vice admiral was returning home after a decisive victory over the German Navy at the Battle of the Falklands on 8 December 1914.

Vice Admiral Frederick Charles Doveton Sturdee at the station.
Hampshire Record Office 217M84/56/55.

1. Wolmar, Christian, *Fire and Steam*, (London, 2007), pp. 207-8.
2. Wolmar, *Fire and Steam*, pp. 218-9.
3. HRO, 217M84/56/55

Vice Admiral Sturdee and a presentation at Droxford. From this and the previous view, he is seen coming down the steps to and standing on the Up platform. As there was no public exit from this platform, except by the footbridge, we may conclude this was a departure scene.   Hampshire Record Office 217M84/50/25.

Fourth Battle Squadron at the Battle of Jutland, fought between 31 May and 1 June 1916 in the North Sea near Denmark, under Admiral Jellicoe. Promoted to Admiral in 1918, Sturdee became Admiral of the Fleet in 1921 and was appointed a Knight Grand Cross of the Order of the Bath the same year. He retired to Camberley, in Surrey, and was buried at Frimley in Surrey in 1925, where his monument includes a cross made of timbers from Nelson's ship, *HMS Victory* [5,6].

In 1915, the Government introduced the Defence of the Realm (Liquid Control) Regulations, restricting the sale of alcohol in areas where there were troops, or where there were munitions, as it was

> expedient for the successful prosecution of the present War that the sale and supply of intoxicating liquor in the respective areas defined and specified in the Schedule hereto should be controlled by the State on the ground that War material is being made, loaded, unloaded and dealt with in transit therein, and that men belonging to His Majesties Naval and Military Forces are assembled therein [7].

The 'Portsmouth area' included Soberton and Hambledon, but not Droxford. Intoxicating liquor could only be sold or supplied in licensed premises in the 'Portsmouth area' between 12.00 noon and 2.30 p.m. and between 6 p.m. and 9 p.m. on weekdays, and between 12.30 p.m. and 2.30 p.m. and between 6 p.m. and 9 p.m. on Sundays. If it was to be consumed off the premises, it could not be sold or taken away after 8 p.m.

Spirits could only be taken off the premises to be consumed from Monday to Friday between 12 noon and 2.30 p.m., but 'licensed premises and refreshment houses' could sell food and non-intoxicating liquor at the pre-war times still permitted in most of the country. No spirits consumed off the premises could be sold or supplied in or taken from any refreshment room in any railway station [8]. It meant that drinking was restricted at the Station Hotel, but not in Droxford.

Strike Action

The early months of the war saw a great increase in the price of food; by January 1915, it rose by about 17 per cent in small towns, and more in large

British ships, under the command of Sturdee, were in Stanley Harbour on 7 December. The following day a German squadron, under Admiral Graf Maximilian von Spee, attempted to raid the British supply base at Stanley. In the battle, 1,871 German sailors were killed, including Admiral von Spee and his two sons, and 215 German survivors were rescued and imprisoned on British ships. Of 765 officers and men on the *Scharnhorst,* only 7 survived. Of the eight German ships, two escaped but were captured in March 1915. The British ships were not seriously damaged: 10 sailors died and 19 were wounded [4].

In January 1916, Sturdee was made a hereditary baronet. He commanded the

4. http://en.wikipedia.org/wiki/Battle_of_the_Falkland_Islands
5. http://janus.lib.cam.ac.uk/db/node.xsp?id=EAD%2FGBR%2F0014%2FSDEE
6. http://en.wikipedia.org/wiki/Doveton_Sturdee
7. *The London Gazette*, 12 November 1915, p. 11172.
8. *The London Gazette*, 12 November 1915, p. 11192.

towns. Even those in rural areas were affected. The price of eggs was 60 per cent higher and fish 51 per cent. By late 1915, with families unable to afford nutritious food, the government gradually increased wages so that, by the end of the war, adult males earned a bonus of 33s a week. A railway porter, who earned 18s a week before the war, was paid 51s a week in February 1919, an increase of 183.3 per cent. The cost of living had risen by 120 to 125 per cent in the same period, and those staff who were paid higher wages and salaries before the war did less well: an express train driver's wage increased from 48s to 81s a week, an increase of only 68.7 per cent[9].

In early 1919, with widespread industrial unrest, the government announced an eight hour day for all railwaymen. Locomotive crews would keep the 33s bonus, and drive no more than 120 miles a day, but the government proposed reductions in pay back to 1913 levels for all other staff, so that a porter earning 51s to 53s a week would in future get 40s. The five minute break allowed in the previous forty years for men to wash their hands at 6.00 am and 1.00 pm was cancelled, and notices to this effect were posted up in railway stations. The unions agreed to demand a 38 hour week, 21 days a year holiday, double pay on public holidays and other changes.

David Lloyd George made a new offer in September 1919: the reduction in wages would be delayed until 1 January 1920, only coming into operation if the cost of living fell below its September 1919's level of 115 per cent over July 1914.

A nine day long strike began at midnight on Friday 26 September, with nearly 200,000 railway men on strike. The Associated Society of Locomotive Engineers and Fireman (ASLEF) supported the National Union of Railwaymen (NUR), which meant a total stoppage, although men continued to feed and water horses voluntarily accompanied by pickets. By 5 October, it had cost the Exchequer £10 million because little goods traffic got through. If railwaymen's wages were lowered, other workers feared theirs would likewise be reduced. The aristocracy and upper classes volunteered to keep the railways running e.g. Lord Louis Mountbatten drove engines for the Isle of Wight Central Railway while Mr Winston Churchill, as Minister of War, ordered units of the armed forces to protect all railway stations, bridges and signal boxes. Servicemen were encouraged to volunteer to work on the railway, with an extra 1s 9d a day for privates to 6s a day for high ranking officers.

Agreement was speedily reached with wages remaining at their existing level until 30 September 1920, no adult railway worker receiving less than 51s a week so long as the cost of living was at least 110 per cent above the pre-war level. The government and the unions agreed no man would be prejudiced for striking, and arrears of wages during the strike would be paid, while the unions stated that strikers would work harmoniously with those who remained at work [10]. It is not known if any at Droxford Station went on strike, but it would have affected them. The number of grades was reduced, and it led to the 1921 Railway Act, the setting up of the Ministry of Transport and the regrouping of the railway companies.

Between the Wars

When the war ended, some hoped that the second track would be laid on the Meon Valley line, the Admiralty having expressed an interest in its strategic importance, but nothing happened. On 24 July 1919, in the House of Commons, Lieutenant-Colonel Campion asked the President of the Board of Trade:

> if his attention has been called to the dissatisfaction caused throughout rural Hampshire by the new railway services, and especially in the Meon Valley district, which combines great inconvenience as to connections, mostly now made impossible, with extreme unpunctuality; and if he will take steps to get the former service restored?

Sir H. Greenwood replied:

> I am sending my honourable and gallant Friend a copy of a letter which I have received from the London and South-Western Railway Company, stating that the question of improving the train services on the Meon Valley line in the autumn is receiving consideration, and explaining their present difficulties in the matter[11].

Economies began: the signal box at Privett Station was closed in 1922. Trains were shorter, reduced from four or six coaches to two coach 'push-pull sets', which usually used small Drummond M7 0-4-4 Tank engines, so that trains ran

9. Bagwell, Philip S., *The Railwaymen: the history of the National Union of Railwaymen*, (London, 1963), pp. 347-56.
10. Bagwell, *Railwaymen*, pp. 375-404.
11. http://hansard.millbanksystems.com/commons/1919/jul/24/meon-valley-railway

between Alton and Fareham without the locomotive having to be turned[12]. There were longer signal blocks and fewer passing loops: it was effectively being run as a single-track branch line rather than a main line. Goods traffic remained the most important source of income, with one north-bound and one south-bound service each day[13]. A local story was told of an engine driver who set rabbit snares down the line from Droxford on the 'down run', and collected the caught rabbits on the return 'up run'[14].

In 1923 the LSWR, and other railway companies in the region, became part of Southern Railways, with Herbert Walker as general manager. The livery became a darker green, with the gilt lettering changed to yellow, and the word 'Southern' on the sides of the water tank, while the locomotive had a black and white lining.

There were further changes when the footbridges were removed at Tisted, Wickham and West Meon. From June 1926 onwards, passengers crossed the line, under the signalman's 'watchful eye', using a break constructed in the platform near to the signal box, and a foot crossing made from sleepers[15]. The footbridge at Droxford was demolished at an unknown date, the foot crossing being at the north end of the platform.

The Races

For most of the nineteenth century, the Hambledon Hunt race course was on Soberton Down, with races usually held in early May. By 1900, a two mile course was established just over a mile east of Brockbridge, the participants ranging from well-known steeple chase jockeys to local farmers. It could be dangerous not only for horses and riders but for spectators: in 1880, a grandstand holding three hundred people collapsed[17]. The school log book records the disruption on race days. With heavy traffic through the village,

parents were afraid to send their children to school. In 1898, one father was knocked down and severely injured by a vehicle coming away from the course[18]. Excursion trains brought spectators from Portsmouth and other places, who walked from Droxford Station to the race course. The Station Hotel and village inns were packed, there was a fair ground, gypsies and sellers of trinkets and cheap goods, and the police station's three cells were kept full[19]. Although the grandstand remains, the races ended about 1930[20].

The Hambledon Hunt sometimes met at the Station Hotel. The railway may have been used to transport hounds as the Hunt's foxhound kennels were in Droxford: 'the pack comprising 45 couples of hounds, hunts on Monday, Wednesday and Saturday; Bishop's Waltham, Waterloo, Hambledon, Botley, Winchester, Southampton and Petersfield are convenient centres; Droxfield is [the] nearest station to the kennels'[21]. (See illustrations page38 and 39.)

Sugar beet became an important local crop and was transported by rail[22]. In July 1939, there were still two freight trains daily from Monday to Saturday, the one from Alton to Fareham reached Droxford at 12.47 p.m. and left at 1.30 pm, and the train from Fareham to Alton at 2.44 p.m., leaving at 3.21 p.m. There were special instructions for those using the stations at Privett and Droxford, because of the steep gradients on certain sections:

> An up goods train must be placed in the siding clear of the running line before shunting work is commenced. If wagons have to be left on the running line for the purpose of running round, the hand brake must be fully applied and wagon brakes pinned down as may be necessary[23].

Although summer excursion trains to the coast remained popular and well-used, a growing number of people had cars or motorcycles, often with sidecars. Increasingly, people were no longer dependent on the railway: in 1927 Harry

12. Stone, R.A., *The Meon Valley Railway*, (Southampton, 1983), p. 56.
13. http://en.wikipedia.org/wiki/Meon_Valley_Railway
14. HRO, 2/7M84/7.
15. Stone, *Meon Valley Railway*, pp. 56-8.
16. Ann Pendred quoting from Ken Ward's booklet, *Droxford in the Meon Valley*.
17. Ann Pendred quoting John Goldsmith's book, *Hambledon*.
18. Ann Pendred: information from the school's log book.
19. Ann Pendred.
20. http://www.hants.gov.uk/hampshiretreasures/vol01/page253.html
21. *Kelly's Directory*, 1927.
22. Tillman, Denis, *The Meon Valley Revisited*, (Bishop's Waltham, 2003), p. 22.
23. D:\SWC Meon Valley Portfolio R9Dpasswork11.htm.

Views of the railway at Droxford up to 1948 are limited. This applies to many branch and cross country services where the restricted train service meant that access by contemporary photographers was difficult to say the least. Here, we see a post-1948 view and, whilst regretfully, the coaches and locomotives may display a British Railways livery, the type of train was typical of that seen on the route for many years: an 'M7' tank engine and pair of non-corridor coaches. The purist will comment that the signals are of the modern 'upper quadrant' type, whilst regretfully the number of passengers was in excess of those usually carried. The service is about to depart from Droxford - next stop West Meon! At the end of the platform behind the lamp post are a number of standard railway warning and trespass notices.

Ray Stone collection

Lashley of Windridge, perhaps the former owner of the Station Hotel, was a 'motor car proprietor' in Droxford. While Arthur George Withers remained a harness maker in Droxford, Anthony Merrington, a cycle agent in the *Kelly's Directory* in 1923 and in 1927, was a 'motor engineer' in 1939, starting a business which is still going over eighty years later.

Some new engines, such as the Maunsell U-Class, were used for summer excursion trains and wagons carrying heavy agricultural goods but, otherwise, the goods services were worked by redundant engines formerly used with main-line passenger trains, such as the Drummond L12s[24].

Local carrier services increased, using motor vehicles, which provided a more flexible door to door service and competitive rates. By 1923, Frederick William Clarke passed through Droxford and Soberton to Portsmouth on Thursdays. Samuel Frederick Seaward from Meonstoke came through Soberton to Fareham market on Mondays and to Portsmouth on Thursdays, while Albert John Payne of Droxford was a 'cartage contractor'. Clarke and Seaward were still carriers in 1935[25]. In the last available directory, in 1939, Clarke had gone, but F. Seaward Ltd still passed through Soberton to Fareham on Mondays[26].

In 1927 Frederick Charles Andrews, who came from Brooklands Park with his wife Isabel, took over the Railway Hotel, during which time it became known as the Station Hotel[27]. A young friend acted as general help and companion before marrying a local man, Mr Searle who worked on the railway after service in World War Two. People did not yet travel half way around the world to take vacations, and people living in Portsmouth were among those who spent their holidays in the hotel. Dances and concerts were held there for local people and visitors. It was advertised in 1927 as a 'commercial and family hotel; parties catered for; garage'. It no longer depended on the railway for its trade. More people had cars, and rural bus services were developing, both being more convenient for villagers.

From probably 1930 to 1939, when trade directories ceased in the war, the hotel

was owned by Edward George and Mildred Vera Harris[28]. Apart from a period in 1935-6, they did not live there, and it was probably occupied by managers. The Maynards, namely Edward Patrick, James Henry and Annie Bridget were there from 1930 to 1933, and Albert and Edith Jane Nancurrow, with William Edward Davis, in 1933-5. Robert Sydney Crook was there from 1936[29].

In 1936, there were still six local trains a day each way, including Saturdays. Passengers could reach Fareham by 9.00 a.m., but the first train to London left at 8.10 a.m. and did not reach Waterloo until 10.24 a.m. Taking the first train up, and the last train back, allowed eight hours in London. The journey was about five to ten minutes slower than in 1914. In July 1939, there were seven train services a day each way, the first down to Fareham and the last up being ordinary trains with a locomotive, rather than push-pull trains. On Sundays, there were three trains each way, between London and Portsmouth[30].

The expectations had been that the Meon Valley Railway would become a main line service, with 600 foot long platforms, with provision for a double track, but the LSWR did not market its potential in its early years. Herbert Walker, appointed in 1912, who became general manager of the Southern Railway from 1923 to 1937, was a shrewd man who would not have seen any reason to spend money developing a country line which would produce little profit, especially as the Southern Railway was investing heavily in developing Southampton as a major liner port, with a good rail service to London.

Services in the Meon Valley were reduced from 1915 and, when the service from Waterloo to Alton was electrified in 1937, it became a self-contained branch still using steam trains. There were no longer through trains to London. R.A. Stone commented that the engines 'looked rather forlorn' standing alongside 600 foot long platforms[31].

24. http://en.wikipedia.org/wiki/Meon_Valley_Railway
25. *Kelly's Directory*, 1923, 1935.
26. *Kelly's Directory*, 1939.
27. HRO, H/CL9/4/317.
28. *Kelly's Directory*, 1931, 1935, 1939.
29. HRO, H/CL9/4/319-28.
30. D:\SWC Meon Valley Portfolio R9D\passwork02.htm
31. Stone, *Meon Valley Railway*, p. 44.

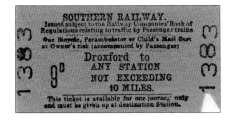

With the outbreak of war in September 1939, troop trains used the line to reach Southampton for embarkation to France, mainly late at night and on Sundays, a box van being added to every train in order to carry extra parcels and the troops' luggage[1]. Officers used the line to reach Portsmouth for, although slower, it was quieter and the scenery more attractive than the main line[2]. Young evacuees arrived by train from Gosport and Portsmouth, to be placed in local homes away from bombing, those in Newtown School and in West Meon coming from Gosport[3].

Unlike in World War One, working for a railway company became a 'reserved' occupation, its employees having to apply if they wanted join the forces. Sixty thousand did so, and women were recruited to fill the gaps: from 25,000 in 1939, there were 105,000 women in 1943 employed as guards, operating signals, portering and cleaning carriages, but not on the footplate[4]. Other men and women were conscripted into the forces and into essential occupations, including the railways and farming.

Reg Gould

Born in the New Forest, he was called up into the army but was released after six months as, shortly before conscription, he qualified as a railway signalman and it was realised that more signalmen were needed. Moving to Droxford Station in 1941, his first reaction was "What god forsaken place have I come to now!"

He was lodging in Brockbridge House with Lew Clarke when he met his future wife Doris, the oldest of four sisters who lived with their parents in a cottage in Meonstoke. They met when Doris went to a regular dance, a village hop, in the

Reg Gould, Signalman at Droxford from 1941 until closure. Together with colleague Bert McRill, both men effectively ran the station, the grade requiring each to be omni competent in every task associated with the operation. Reg's reaction upon being sent to Droxford by the Southern Railway was, "What god forsaken place have I come to now!" In the background is the wind pump used to draw water for the station.

1. Stone, R.A., *The Meon Valley Railway*, (Southampton, 1983), p. 69.
2. Information from Adrian Falks.
3. Ann Pendred.
4. Wolmar, Christian, *Fire and Steam*, (London, 2007), pp. 244-5.

hall behind the Station Hotel, with her sister Eileen and a friend. Eileen, a paper girl, collected the daily newspapers from Droxford Station each morning and sorted them out, so she knew Reg. Spotting a ring on Doris's finger, he commented "Not another married or engaged", whereupon Doris explained that it was just a dress ring with no such significance[5]. During and after the war, social life continued at the Station Hotel where, in the hall at the back, there was a dance floor. Pantomimes were held there, and it had a cinema with a hand cranked projector[6].

She was in domestic service at The Grove in Droxford but, at the age of nineteen, had to choose whether to work in a factory or join the Land Army. Choosing the former, Doris went to work in a factory at Winton near Bournemouth where she was trained as an aircraft fitter and worked on Stirling bombers. Every other weekend, Reg visited her in Bournemouth where she lived in digs and, alternate weekends, she came home to her family and saw him. In Bournemouth she narrowly missed a German bombing raid, after which she was sent home to recover from shock, and subsequently became engaged to Reg[7].

John Moon left school in 1941 aged fourteen, and worked at Parkers Farm in Hambledon from 1941 until 1951:

> At Parkers, I often had to visit the goods yard at Droxford Station. Reg Gould used to supply a wagon for us to load. It was mostly sugar beet. If possible we preferred to load the wagon from the goods platform as the railway wagon was very high and difficult to load from track level. We also collected supplies from the goods yard including barley from Newcastle which was used for beer (it came in 2cwt sacks) and farm fertiliser from Fisons which arrived in ten ton trucks (also in 2cwt bags)[8].

Doris Gould recalled that Reg was very active around the station and would load and unload goods, particularly sugar beet[9].

For safety reasons, train speeds were reduced to 30 mph for passenger trains and 10 mph for goods trains, as materials and people to maintain the track were in short supply. Slow speeds often caused the service to grind to a halt. All lights were turned off in the coaches, apart from a faint blue light, until hooded lamps and effective blinds could be installed. Fares remained the same throughout the war, but trains were overcrowded and often delayed as those carrying troops had priority. In 1944, an average of 500 troop trains ran each day leading up to the preparations for D-Day[10].

Land girls arrived to work in the district, and local service men would leave home from Droxford Station. Petrol rationing would mean that people in rural areas returned to horses for transport and haulage, and train travel[11]. Miss Barbara Wade used her governess cart, pulled by her horse Rufus, to take passengers and luggage between Droxford and the station[12].

The line carried goods and equipment for the naval dockyard at Portsmouth. In 1941, a military train travelled from Swallowcliffe to the coast, part of an experiment to transport troops and transport together: six coaches, carrying troops, and thirty-five Bren Gun carriers on flat bogie wagons, hauled by a Drummond 700 class 'Black Motor' engine, spent two days in the long siding at Droxford, and were delayed for several hours by 'vacuum trouble'. It is not known if the stay at Droxford was planned, or how the troops were fed, watered and toileted. That same year, another train spent the night in sidings at Tisted; two days later, the train's crew and the station staff learnt that it carried forty-eight mines.

The Germans wanted to destroy communication routes, particularly those leading to the coast and, in 1940, a Junkers 88 aeroplane flew up the Meon Valley. It dropped bombs either side of the line at Soberton, missing the line, and at Droxford Station, where they caused light damage to the station buildings, and demolished two of the railway cottages, but nobody was injured. It flew over West Meon Station before dropping another bomb intended to destroy the north entrance to the tunnel at West Meon. It missed but destroyed

5. Mrs Doris Gould's recollections recorded by Tony Williams in October 2011.
6. John Moon's recollections recorded by Tony Williams in 2010.
7. Mrs Doris Gould.
8. John Moon.
9. Mrs Doris Gould.
10. Wolmar, *Fire and Steam*, pp. 257-9.
11. John Moon.
12. Ward, Kenneth, *Droxford in the Meon Valley*, (Havant)

Possibly Droxford in early June 1944. Front row, left to right: Mr Mackenzie King (Prime Minister - Canada), Mr Winston Churchill, Mr Peter Fraser (Prime Minister - New Zealand), General Eisenhower, Sir Godfrey Huggins (Prime Minister - Southern Rhodesia), General Smuts (Prime Minister - South Africa and confidant of Churchill). Post-war, a framed copy of this photograph hung in the booking office at Droxford but disappeared after closure in 1955 (the frame had been made at Eastleigh). The original was later presented to Mr Charles Anderson MBE from the area control office of the Southern Railway at Southampton who had suggested and made arrangements for the use of Droxford. (Although the image has been widely attributed to Droxford Station, there are real doubts that it was taken there. The platforms details do not appear correct and there is no record of General Eisenhower visiting the station. The premiers did attend the 1944 Commonwealth Prime Ministers Conference in London from 1 May to 16 May, most returning to their home countries soon after. They and Churchill would have met with General Eisenhower around that time. it has been suggested that it was taken on 12 May when Churchill, Eisenhower and Commonwealth premiers visited Coastal Artillery sites.)

Crown Copyright.

sleepers and part of the track, damaging Vinnells Lane Bridge. A telephone call was made to Privett Station in time to halt the 4.30 p.m. train passenger train from Alton. After repairs, the line was soon in action again[13].

Reg Gould was on duty in the signal box at Droxford Station when a stick of bombs was dropped on the line while a freight train was being shunted, but there was only shrapnel damage resulting in a few holes in brickwork[14]. He escaped both bombing and machine gunning by the German plane[15].

Mr McLeod was station master at Droxford during the war[16]. A woman was employed in the ticket office until she married in 1949[17]. The station, including the signal box, was manned twenty-four hours a day; Reg Gould worked a twelve hour shift and, when off duty, served in the Home Guard. It was initially proposed that he and Doris would live in one of the surviving two railway cottages, but this proved impossible and they lived in Meonstoke[18].

D Day

Winston Churchill recalled that, in 1944, 'On the morning of Friday, June 2nd I set off in my train for our siding by Eisenhower's Headquarter's at Portsmouth

13. HRO, 2/7M84/8.
14. D:\SWC Meon Valley Portfolio R9D\locoworking05.htm
15. Mrs Doris Gould.
16. D:\SWC Meon Valley Portfolio R9D\staff01.htm. It is not known where he lived, as directories and electoral rolls were not printed during the war.
17. Reg Daniels' recollections recorded by Tony Williams in November 2011.
18. Mrs Doris Gould.

with Field Marshall Smuts, Mr Ernest Bevin, General Ismay and my personal staff . . .'[19].

That day, a telephone call was sent down the line from each tablet section, with instructions that the main line was to be kept clear of trains in order to allow free passage to a special train, the royal train belonging to the London, Midland and Scotland Railway, consisting of six pristine red coaches hauled by a Drummond T9 engine[20]. On arrival at Droxford Station, it drew into the sidings where an additional engine was positioned there, in case of emergencies, and a mess van. A special telephone line was laid on, a Southern Region inspector from Waterloo was present, and the station and sidings were guarded by troops from nearby camps[21]. It was said locally that, if there was an air raid, the train could be easily pushed into the deep cutting just south of the station.

It was supposed to be secret but, within an hour of its arrival, everyone in Droxford knew, but kept it secret. Mr McIntosh, the post master, could only let official mail leave the village during the four days that the train was there[22]. Mr Reg Gould was on duty, and was provided with a special breakfast which was off ration. His daughter had been born in May 1944[23].

For months Operation Overlord, the invasion of Normandy, had been planned and Winston Churchill was using this train as his base, to be as near as possible to the coast. Field-Marshall Jan Smuts, prime minister of South Africa, and General 'Pug' Ismay remained with him. When Churchill became prime minister in 1940, he appointed Ismay as his chief military assistant and staff officer, serving as the principal link between Churchill and the Chiefs of Staff Committee. A secretary, Marion Holmes was on the train for the whole period. General Eisenhower, Supreme Commander of the Allied Forces, was nearby at Southwick House.

On the morning of 3 June, Anthony Eden, Foreign Secretary and Leader of the House of Commons, and Pierson Dixon, Eden's principal secretary, arrived to hear the prime minister bathing. In his autobiography, Dixon wrote that it

looked like any country station apart from C.I.D. men discreetly hidden in the booking-office. One or two C.I.D. men strolled about the platform, one of whom escorted them along the railway line where,

> . . after 200 yards, round a curve, we came to the train. It consisted of two saloons: one with a bedroom at one end and a tiny office and telephone at the other; the other saloon doing service as dining-room and conference room[24].

Eden described the train as 'an imaginative but uncomfortable exercise on Mr Churchill's part. Accommodation was limited and there was only one bath, adjoining his own compartment, and one telephone. Mr Churchill seemed to be always in the bath and General Ismay always on the telephone'.

Although it was close to the action, '. . . it was almost impossible to conduct any business'[25]. Duff Cooper, a member of the War Cabinet, called it 'a perfectly absurd scheme'[26].

Eden and Dixon looked at a box from the Foreign Office, had a drink, and then drove to Eton to meet relatives, have a picnic lunch with Dixon's son in his room at Eton College, watch the 'Procession of the Boats' on the Thames, stroll about the cricket pitch and drive back to the train at Droxford[27].

On the train, Ernest Bevin returned at lunchtime and, after a meal, the train took Churchill, Smuts and Bevin to Southampton to watch the troops embark, before taking a motor launch to Portsmouth. A torpedo boat MTB 102 carried Churchill and General Eisenhower to review the D-Day fleet, including landing craft, which Churchill described as 'wonderful sights to see with all these thousands of vessels' when he telegraphed President Roosevelt the following day. They visited General Eisenhower's headquarters on the way back to the train.

The train arrived back at Droxford Station at 8.00 p.m., where Eden and Dixon were waiting at the siding. Dixon noted that

> PM arrived accompanied by Smuts, Bevin, Geoffrey-Lloyd, Duncan Sandys, Pug Ismay and Tommy Thompson. After he had changed from his Trinity House uniform to the cooler drill of a Colonel of the Hussars, we had a very convivial dinner in the dining saloon. It was a very pictorial scene – the two old warlords [Churchill and Smuts], fat, gross Ernie Bevin and Anthony, very elegant, next to him, and the

19. *Droxford: A Hampshire Village its History and its Church*, pp. 18-9.
20. On single lines, to ensure no other locomotive was on the line, the driver collected the tablet for that section from the side of the track before he entered.
21. HRO, 2/7M84/7
22. *Droxford: A Hampshire Village*, pp. 18-9.
23. Mrs Doris Gould.
24. Dixon, Piers, *Double Diploma, The Life of Sir Pierson Dixon, Don and Diplomat*, (London, 1963), p. 89.
25. Eden, Anthony, *The Eden Memoirs: Volume Two: The Reckoning*, (London, 1965), p. 452.
26. Beevor, Anthony, *D Day*, (London, 2009), p. 19.
27. Dixon, *Double Diploma*, p. 89.

lesser fry at the ends of the narrow table. The food was admirable, with 1926 champagne and a grand old brandy out of balloon glasses[28].

These were Churchill's most trusted colleagues. When, in 1940, Churchill formed an all-party coalition government, he appointed Ernest Bevin, a Labour M.P. and trade unionist as Minister for Labour and National Service. The illegitimate child of a village midwife, Bevin could not have had a more different upbringing to Anthony Eden, now seen as Churchill's natural successor, who was educated at Eton. Eden was often called upon to restrain Churchill's ideas, but one which went ahead was the unexpected but successful choice of Bevin, an appointment which secured the support of British workers.

Geoffrey William Geoffrey-Lloyd, a Conservative M.P. was the minister in charge of the Petroleum Warfare Department; Duncan Sandys, Churchill's son-in-law, was a minister and chairman of a War Cabinet Committee concerned with the defence against German flying bombs and rockets, while Commander C. R. 'Tommy' Thompson RN was one of Churchill's most trusted aides. A flag lieutenant at the Admiralty, Thompson's main role was to organise the prime minister's journeys, both at home and overseas, including the stay at Droxford Station.

Eden and Bevin

Those at dinner on the train talked mainly about British and South African politics about the time of the Boer War. Bevin and Eden sat together and, as the drink flowed, tongues loosened and, according to Dixon,

> . . . the P.M. very genial. E. Bevin, who likes Anthony, became very affectionate towards him [Eden] at their end of the evening, and their friendliness provoked the P.M. to say he was ready to give up the leadership to either, or both of them, at any time[29].

Eden and Bevin talked of 'the impending battle and then of the political future'. The former gained the impression that Bevin thought it might be necessary for the National Government to continue into the post-war period, as Bevin asked Eden if he knew what Churchill intended. Eden said that he did not, whereupon Bevin replied that 'if the old man retired', he was sure the two of them could

work together, if it was the right thing to do. Bevin thought it would not present any difficulties for him: he would not care which office either of them held. Eden said, 'Neither would I.' but Bevin replied that there was one which he must have, which was the nationalisation of the coalmines, as the trade unions would have to see that happen.

Later, Smuts asked Eden what the two had talked about for so long. When Eden told him, Smuts 'commented with characteristic crispness, 'cheap at the price'[30]. However, one absentee at Droxford was Clement Attlee, leader of the Labour Party, and deputy prime minister since 1942, who would sweep to power in the general election in 1945 and become prime minister with Bevin as Foreign Secretary. Bevin's opposition to Soviet expansion was to dissatisfy Labour's left, but won the approval of the Conservative Opposition led by Churchill. Many considered Bevin would made a better prime minister than Attlee, but Bevin died in 1951, and Eden would succeed Churchill as prime minister.

General de Gaulle

Control of the D-Day landings and the invasion of France lay with the President of the United States and General Eisenhower who, on the night of 3 June, postponed the operation for at least twenty-four hours because of deteriorating weather. The new date would be 6 June, when there would be a short period of better weather. Ismay took the telephone call in the early hours of 4 June and, soon afterwards, Churchill summoned him and was informed of the change in plans.

The War Cabinet had previously discussed its future relationship with General de Gaulle, agreeing that he be invited to England from Algiers and informed by Churchill, on 4 June, about D-Day. Churchill had informed President Roosevelt that it might otherwise 'become a very great insult to France'. However, no communication was to be allowed between the Free French in London and de Gaulle's base in Algiers[31].

Eden and Dixon spent the night of 3 to 4 June at Eden's house at Binderton, as the train's facilities were too cramped to work[32]. They arrived after midnight, and met the American Ambassador who had come down from London to see

28. Gilbert, Martin, *Winston S. Churchill: Volume Seven: Road to Victory 1941-1945*, vol. 7, (London, 1986), p. 787. *The Times*, 19 January 2012.
29. Dixon, *Double Diploma*, p. 90.
30. Eden, *Eden Memoirs: Volume Two*, pp. 453-4.
31. Gilbert, *Winston S. Churchill: Volume Seven*, p. 786
32. Eden, *Eden Memoirs: Volume Two*, p. 453.

(272)

IN THE TRAIN

THE CHARTWELL TRUST

4 June, 1944.

TOP SECRET

My dear General de Gaulle,

   Welcome to these shores! Very great military events are about to take place. I should be glad if you could come to see me down here in my train, which is close to General Eisenhower's Headquarters, bringing with you one or two of your party. General Eisenhower is looking forward to seeing you again and will explain to you the military position which is momentous and imminent. If you could be here by 1.30 p.m., I should be glad to give you dejeuner and we will then repair to General Eisenhower's Headquarters. Let me have a telephone message early to know whether this is agreeable to you or not.

                    Yours sincerely,

                         (Signed) WINSTON S. CHURCHILL.

Monsieur le General de Gaulle.

Eden. The ambassador stayed until 2.00 a.m. before returning to London, promising to contact the President who still opposed Churchill's advances to de Gaulle[33].

Churchill wrote to de Gaulle as opposite[34].

Versions of the morning of Sunday 4 June differ. According to Dixon, they returned to the train and were soon joined by Tedder, the Deputy Allied Supreme Commander, and others to discuss the weather and the decision to postpone the Normandy Landings. About midday, they walked along the railway line to meet de Gaulle, who soon appeared and looked surprised to be greeted by the Foreign Secretary at a small station[35].

Having flown into Northolt, according to Martin Gilbert, De Gaulle arrived at Droxfield Station shortly before 1.00 p.m[36]. Eden, arriving about the same time, walked down the line with him towards Churchill, who greeted de Gaulle on the track with arms outstretched. Eden thought that de Gaulle may have felt 'genuinely uncertain' about this strange meeting on a train and was offended that no agreement had yet been made about the future civil administration of France. President Roosevelt had refused to permit discussions between the United States, Great Britain and France.

Smuts and Bevin were present when Churchill told de Gaulle about the intended invasion. When de Gaulle raised the issue of the future administration of France, Churchill suggested that de Gaulle should ask to visit Roosevelt, and told the General that, if there was no agreement between France and the United States, Churchill would side with President Roosevelt. Both Eden and Bevin were unhappy with the way Churchill handled the situation, and Eden wrote that 'The meeting was a failure'.

Eden managed a few quiet words with de Gaulle in which he tried to rectify the earlier meeting with Churchill, stressing to de Gaulle that General Eisenhower had always wanted to work with the

33. Dixon, *Double Diploma*, p. 90.
34. The Sir Winston Churchill Archive Trust, CHAR 20/137C.
35. Dixon, *Double Diploma*, p. 91.
36. Gilbert, *Winston S. Churchill: Volume Seven*, p. 788.

French Committee of National Liberation. Churchill and de Gaulle drove to see General Eisenhower at Southwick House.

De Gaulle was asked to comment on Eisenhower's declaration to the French people, but the printed declaration had already been printed and failed to include de Gaulle's comments, which further upset him[37]. With the United States in control of the Allied invasion, Churchill's role was to inform de Gaulle, but it had been a badly handled meeting which probably contributed towards de Gaulle's veto, on two occasions, of Britain's membership of the EEC. He insisted that Britain end her special relationship with both the Commonwealth and the United States. If Churchill's discussion with de Gaulle at Droxford Station had been successful, and he and Attlee had resigned at the end of the war, the future of post-war Britain could have been very different.

The special train left Droxford at 5.56 p.m. on Sunday 5 June on its way to Waterloo. Churchill returned to 10 Downing Street where, in the Annexe, the duty typist was called in at 10.30 p.m. until 3.45 a.m. She wrote that 'He drives himself too hard and he nearly fell asleep over the papers'[38].

The Home Guard

John Moon, aged seventeen in 1944, was the youngest member of the local Home Guard, for which he was paid 3s a day. In 2010, he recalled those days before D-Day:

On Friday 2nd June 1944 I was on duty to guard the railway bridge at Droxford Station We were based at the Station Hotel. I cycled there with my workmate to be on duty by 22:00 hours. Unknown to me Mr Churchill and others had come down from London in a special train and had been shunted into the goods yard for the night. We did the first guard duty from 22:00 hours to 24:00. We were told to keep alert but in our duty period we saw nobody and nothing moving. The next guard was from 24:00 hours to 02:00 hours. They moved to the top of the

bridge (we had been under the bridge). This meant that the guard who went on duty at 02:00 hours had to walk through the station gates and walk up to the line to the bridge to change guard. At 01:55 the quartermaster sergeant (QMS) and two guards marched through the Station Hotel forecourt, across Station Road and towards the station gates. A Canadian Major inside the station gates approached and both the Major and the QMS pulled their pistols and challenged "Halt. Who goes there?" at exactly the same time. No one answered and the two privates became worried that the Major would shoot them. Luckily the Major broke the silence by asking what they were doing and was told that they were guarding the bridge. The Major asked "You are not guarding Mr Churchill?" and the QMS replied "No, only the bridge".

The Major asked to be taken to the Home Guards' officer, a very deaf eighty year old Colonel, so John Moon and his fellow Home Guard member could hear the conversation: 'The outcome was we were to carry on with what we were doing and to keep out of their way as Mr Churchill had plenty of guards. We were happy to oblige and at 06:00 we went home.'

The next day, Saturday 3 June, when John Moon went to Bishops Waltham to get a permit for his flash light, he saw Mr Churchill in a car with an outrider going towards Southampton. Being a paper boy, on Sunday 4 June, he went to Droxford Station to collect the papers from the up train: 'I saw Mr Churchill's train in the goods yard opposite the Station House and I could see General Smuts having a wash. The train was brown in colour.[39]'

Ron Crook, billeted at the Station Hotel, was the sergeant in charge of the Swanmore platoon of the Home Guard on guard duty at Droxford Railway Station in the early days of June 1944. He recalled that, on the evening of 2 June, a large locomotive drew into the station and later that night, in the hotel, the officer in charge of the platoon told him 'in a slightly hysterical tone':

37. Eden, *Eden Memoirs: Volume Two*, pp. 452-3.
38. Gilbert, *Winston S. Churchill: Volume Seven*, p. 790.
39. John Moon.

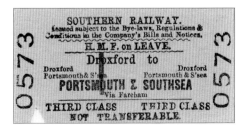

Left - *Droxford Home Guard, recorded in front of Fir Hill House, Droxford. Back row, left to right: Jack Horn, Dicky Osborn, Unknown, Unknown, Unknown, Bert Carter, Vic Turner, Bill Pearcey, Harry Blunden, Unknown, Unknown. Middle row, left to right: Unknown, John Moon, Tom Pink, Mr Webb, Unknown, George Cannings, Mr Harriet, Ern Pearce, Mr Wilsmere. Front row, left to right: Mrs Adams, Corporal Ted Adams, Sergeant Etheridge, Lieut. Adams, Lieut. Harriot, Quartermaster Sergeant Etheridge, Corporal Tom Rigg, Corporal May.*

John Moon collection.

"There is a rumour that Churchill will be here tonight, and if you see him report to me immediately, but don't panic!".

According to Ron Crook, the next day (4 June) he saw two men out strolling, one of whom was vaguely familiar: a small man with a pointed beard, whom he recognised as General Smuts, who introduced him to General de Gaulle, 'a tall, angular individual in a foreign uniform' who

> . . . remained aloof and said nothing and they moved off in the direction of the train. A few minutes later, all hell broke loose! The Special

Forces and Royal Marine Commandos who had been guarding the train were swarming around me in panic as they had "lost" two Generals. I reassured them that they'd returned to the train[40]!

Not surprisingly, many more boasted in the local pubs of having seen Churchill. According to Ann Pendred, 'one man had no such story but, not to be outdone, his claim was to have emptied Churchill's toilet bucket!!!!'.

On 6 June, D-Day, Allied forces landed on the Normandy beaches. The invasion of mainland Europe had begun. World War Two ended in 1945. Most

40. http://www.bbc.co.uk/ww2peopleswar/stories/46/a3394046.shtml

servicemen came back safely, compared with World War One: four men from Soberton, including Serjeant Harry Oswald Leggett MM of the Royal Artillery and Reginald Percy Tanner DSC, Commander of HMS Gloucester, and eleven from Droxford, failed to survive and are remembered on the war memorials.

Soon after, Churchill lost the General Election. A Labour Government, with Clement Attlee as prime minister, came into power and, on 1 January 1948, the railways were nationalised. Southern Railways became part of British Railways, the business name of the Railway Executive of the British Transport Commission.

DROXFORD STATION

In a special train at this station, the Rt.Hon. Sir Winston Churchill MP then Prime Minister of the UK spent some days making crucial decisions with his staff prior to the invasion of Europe on D Day 6th June 1944

Above - The plaque installed outside Droxford Station in June 2012 to mark Churchill's visit. (This replaced an earlier version.)

Right - 'Walking in the footsteps of history'. In August 1950 six years after Churchill's visit, 'Picture Post' sent their photographer Bert Hardy to revisit the scene. In what is clearly a posed view, Porter / Signalmen Bert McRill (left) and Reg Gould, who were on duty on the occasion in June 1944, are seen walking on to the up siding where the train was held. The single line over which service trains would pass is on the right. (As might be expected with a press visit, it was normal for more than one image to be recorded and having located this view there were high hopes for others of the station of a similar quality taken at the same time. Unusually it was unique.) A note on the back of the file print within the archive also records two simple words, 'Story Killed'. Perhaps just six years after the event it was still meant to be Droxford's secret. Getty Archive 98087991

8
THE END OF THE LINE

As life gradually returned to normal and petrol rationing eased, people of all social classes began to buy their own cars, there was a regular bus service along the Meon Valley, and people travelled less by train. There were cheap day return train tickets to London, but people had to get the 6.57 p.m. train from Waterloo in order to catch the last train from Alton to Fareham, and railway stations were sited some way from villages. Cars were more convenient than trains, whose carriages were often in a poor state, while the condition of many stations had been neglected since long before the war. The track and rolling stock were in a poor state, and there was a considerable increase in railway accidents.

In 1951, the Sunday passenger rain service was cut out and, soon after, the weekday service was reduced to four trains in each direction. Trains carrying schoolchildren to and from school are thought to have had four carriages, to allow for extra passengers. Cheap day return tickets continued, but the last train now left Alton at 4.30 p.m. For those with cars, there were free parking space in towns, even in central London during the day, and yellow lines were yet to be painted on roads. Rail freight charges increased, and more goods began to be carried by road, although British Road Services worked with British Railways and had depots at stations.

Throughout the country, many lines failed to make a profit, and British Railways recorded an operating loss in 1955. In its 'Modernisation Plan', steam locomotives would be withdrawn, main lines electrified, unprofitable services reduced and the least successful branch lines closed. In 1953, the incoming Conservative Government transferred the control of British Railways directly to the British Transport Commission.

Droxford no longer had its own station master; Mr W.E. Squire, station master at Wickham was in charge of Droxford Station. Reg Daniels, the senior porter at Droxford was responsible for the office work, while Reg Gould, present during the D-Day episode, and Harold Dudman, who lived in Soberton, were

signalmen, while one of the two remaining railway cottages was occupied by one of the platelayer's gang[1].

Reg Daniels

Born in Meonstoke and having lived in Soberton, Reg Daniels worked at Droxford Railway Station from 1949 to 1955, his first job on the railway. He started after demobilisation following the Second World War, having being told by the station master at West Meon of a vacancy at Droxford Station, as the woman who ran the office during the war was getting married. After four to five weeks training by the station master at West Meon, he would handle a wide range of duties including ticket sales, livestock and goods transport, indeed everything except for the signal box. Mr Squire from Wickham came to Droxford once or twice a week to check on the paperwork etc., and there were two signalmen, including Reg Gould, who worked a day shift. The station master at West Meon controlled the stations north of West Meon.

The goods yard was very active, mostly dealing with sugar beet and farm supplies including fertiliser. There was quite a volume of parcels including perishable goods for the local stores, and a reasonable number of passengers,

1. HRO, 2/7M84/7; Reg Daniels' recollections recorded by Tony Williams in November 2011.

some of whom used the station for trips to London. Strawberries were loaded at Wickham and Swanwick.

J. E. Smith still had a coal yard at the station and delivered locally while Ray Stone's father, Peter Stone, ran the coal yard at West Meon and also traded in Droxford. The station building at Droxford was let out during his time to Westbrook's, a decorating firm, and Horace Weyman, who worked at Westbrook's, rented out the house for 19 shillings a week[2].

Year	Occupants eligible to vote
1945	Elsie Parker, Violet Thornton. Lewis A. Thornton and Horace D. Weyman were listed there but on the Service Register, as they were away serving in the forces.
1946	No register
1947-65	Elsie Parker, Horace D. and Ethel Weyman
1966-1972	Horace D. and Ethel Weyman
1973	No one listed

Occupants of the Station House from 1945 to 1973, taken from the electoral registers[3].

Year	3 Railway Cottages	4 Railway Cottages
1945		Richard Carter
1947-1964	Fred G. & Eleanor E. Boyes	Richard & Lilian F. Carter
1965-1972	Fred G. & Eleanor E. Boyes; from 1970, David Boyes also had a vote	?empty

Heads of household of the Railway Cottages at Droxford Station taken from the electoral registers 1945-1973[4]. In 1973, no one appears to be living in the railway cottages.

On 3 May 1954, the British Transport Commission (BTC) wrote to the Chairman of Droxford Rural District Council (Droxford RDC) that a review of the economic circumstances of the Meon Valley Line had revealed 'a serious financial situation'. It proposed the withdrawal of passenger services between Alton and Fareham, and the complete closure of the line between Farringdon and Droxford, leaving only freight services between Alton and Farringdon (3½ miles) and Fareham and Droxford (9¾ miles). The existing single line was 23½ miles long, Droxford being 16 miles from Alton. Thirteen miles of the middle section of the line would be closed[5]. It was suggested that Petersfield, Medstead and Ropley Stations were within reasonable distance, and might be convenient to certain users.

Collection and delivery services for freight train traffic and parcels traffic would continue with 'facilities for truckload traffic for cartage by the public' remaining at Farringdon, Droxford, Mislingford Siding and Wickham. The existing passenger platform at Droxford Station would be available as 'a dock for handling sugar beet and other agricultural produce, so improving the freight facilities at this point'.

The BTC, having considered the railway's future prospects, taking into consideration that freight train traffic mainly consisted of agricultural produce and supplies, and domestic coal, concluded that:

> The area served by the line is entirely rural, and having regard to the provisions of the County Development Plan, it is not considered that any developments are likely to take place in the vicinity which would offer sufficient potential traffic to justify retention of the passenger service, or of the freight service on the portion of the line considered for complete closure.

The BTC proposed that, subject to the approval of the licensing authority, Southdown Motor Service Ltd.'s bus route 38, from Portsmouth to Meonstoke, be increased to six trips each way each day, which would cover the previous train service and provide a service later in the day. Hampshire County Council objected to the BTC's proposals. At a meeting in Alton Urban District Council's

2. Reg Daniels.
3. HRO, H/CL9/4/329-58.
4. HRO, H/CL9/4/329-58.
5. *The Railway Magazine*, Notes and News, January 1955, p. 65. Other lines were being closed, including 9¾ miles between Petersfield and Midhurst on the Petersfield-Midhurst-Pulborough line on the same day.

Droxford Station forecount, 1 January 1955. The three posters provide detail of the train service, extol the virtues of Guernsey as a holiday destination and ominously, announce closure of the line.

The Lens of Sutton collection

Chambers on 18 June 1954 Mr. Spillard, on behalf of the BTC, announced that four passenger trains a day would be replaced by six journeys on bus route 38, which was expected to save £38,000 a year.

Parking facilities could be arranged at the stations for passengers now 'compelled' to use the proposed bus service, which would be permanent 'but will of course be subject to review from time to time in common with other routes'. The closures would happen, but no firm commitment could be made about alternative bus services in the future.

Mr Petley, a local resident, drew attention to the strain on loading facilities at Droxford and other stations, asking if they could be increased sufficiently. Estimating that an extra 24 wagons a day would be needed at Droxford, he

foresaw grave difficulties, but Mr Spillard was satisfied they could make 'adequate' facilities available although he realised longer runs would be necessary. If there was an increased demand, it 'would be pleased to consider' improving loading facilities at Farringdon, Droxford and Ropley and, wherever the line was open, provision could be made for horse boxes or cattle trucks[6].

The BTC suggested the possibility of a more frequent goods service between Droxford and Fareham, if it was necessary for the conveyance of cattle and other farm animals to the slaughter house at Fareham. Alton RDC felt that the closure would lead to 'an unavoidable drift of population from rural to urban areas, and that it should remain open for goods traffic, even if the passenger service was withdrawn'[7].

6. HRO, 78M73/DDC122: correspondence between Droxford RDC and other re the disuse of the Meon Valley railway.
7. TNA, RAIL 1005/376.

THE ELEMENTS - JANUARY 1955

During the first week of January 1955 much of the country was blanketed in snow, ranging in depth from 4" to 12", Under such conditions the then Medical Officer of Health for Winchester, Dr J L Farmer, ventured out to record the scene at Droxford, picturing not just what was an inhospitable landscape but also the arrival of an Alton bound freight train, later passed by a 'push-pull' service bound for Fareham. Trains south on the Meon Valley line had for many years operated from Alton through Fareham and on to Gosport. This came to an end with the closure of the Fareham - Gosport section to passengers in 1953. Gosport being left with the dubious distinction that it was for many years the largest town in the country to be devoid of railway communication.

Few people now came by train to stay at the Station Hotel. It is not known who owned the hotel but, Melville D. and Grace C. Fritchley lived there in late 1945, while Robert G.K. Dee, a service man, gave it as his home address.

Year	Occupants
1945	Melville D. & Grace C. Fritchely Robert G.K. Dee (Service Register)
1946	No electoral register
1947-9	Robert G.K. & Elizabeth Dee Eveline V. Fox Albert Gates
1949-52	Arthur S. & Beryl L. Littlefield
1953	No names recorded - ?empty
1954-7	Arthur K & Virginia R. Bishop
1958-65	Walter N. & Constance B. Brown. Known as the Railway Hotel.
1966-73	Charles W. & Hilda R. Crook. Known as the Meon Valley Hotel.

Adults over the age of twenty-one living at the hotel, taken from the electoral registers 1945-1973[8].

The future

On 17 November 1954, the BTC informed Droxford RDC that, as 'facilities for traffic to be carted by the public' were available at Alton, Farringdon, Droxford, Mislingford, Wickham, Fareham and Petersfield, the passenger service, and freight between Farringdon and Droxford, would be withdrawn from 7 February 1955.

Alton RDC reported, on 23 November, that Southdown Motor Services Ltd. had not yet applied to the licensing authority to run the new service but, six days later, the bus company replied that plans were well advanced to extend the 38 bus route from Droxford to Alton on 6 February, with buses stopping at The Square in Droxford, and that they would apply to the licensing authority. On 16 December,

8. HRO, H/CL9/4/329-8.

Right - *Closure notice.*   *Norman Simmons*

Left - Fareham train leaving Droxford. The two-coach service is passing the long siding south of the station ('up siding No. 1') on the plan opposite. It was on this siding that Churchill's train had been stabled. In later years, spare main line coaching stock was stored at Droxford and elsewhere over the winter period. Springtime would see such vehicles taken to Eastleigh for servicing prior to being returned to service. No trouble with vandalism at that time! The concrete sleepers will be noted.

Lens of Sutton

***Opposite** - What may well be the original signal diagram from Droxford signal box, removed upon closure and found years later. There were 24 levers. The thick lines indicate passenger running lines.*

Pat Butler

Droxford Parish Council was concerned that the proposed 'omnibus' would be inadequate, and that an express service was necessary. On New Year's Eve, the bus company assured them that an express service was planned between Droxford, Alton, Aldershot and London[9]. The passenger service was due to close in five weeks time. The following March, *The Railway Magazine* reported that the district was well served with buses, but the service did not last long[10].

In January 1955, the National Union of Farmers objected to the closure, stressing the importance of the line during the sugar beet harvest. The Transport Users Committee had a public enquiry, which came out in favour of the closure, and the chairman of Droxford RDC reported that the contract to lift the track had been given by December 1954. According to Reg Daniels, Dr. Richard Beeching, who would become chairman of the new British Railways Board in 1961 and wield the 'Beeching Axe', visited Droxford Station early in 1955. As

for Reg Daniels, he left the railway in 1955 when passenger services stopped and joined Associated British Combustion as an engineer[11].

Now that it was closing, people rushed to buy tickets, use the line, and take photographs[12]. As there was no service on a Sunday, the last normal passenger service ran on Saturday 5 February, 1955.

The special train

The Railway Correspondence and Travel Society arranged a tour of the Meon Valley line and the Petersfield-Midhurst-Pulborough line, as the section between Petersfield and Midhurst was closing at the same time.

On Sunday 6 February, a specially chartered train, *The Hampshireman* left

9. HRO, 78M73/DDC122.
10. *The Railway Magazine*, Notes and News, March 1955, p. 212: 'a main road runs close to the station for almost the whole way and the district is well served with buses.
11. Reg Daniels.
12. Stone, R.A., *The Meon Valley Railway*, (Southampton, 1983), pp. 94-5.

BRITISH RAILWAYS — SOUTHERN REGION
DROXFORD

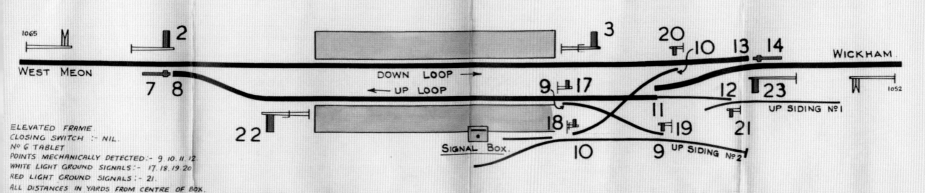

WEST MEON

DOWN LOOP →

← UP LOOP

WICKHAM

SIGNAL BOX.

DOWN LOOP

UP SIDING Nº 1

UP SIDING Nº 2

ELEVATED FRAME.
CLOSING SWITCH :- NIL.
Nº 6 TABLET
POINTS MECHANICALLY DETECTED :- 9. 10. 11. 12.
WHITE LIGHT GROUND SIGNALS :- 17. 18. 19. 20.
RED LIGHT GROUND SIGNALS :- 21.
ALL DISTANCES IN YARDS FROM CENTRE OF BOX.

MECHANICAL LOCKING   ELECTRICAL LOCKING & DETECTION.

DISTANCES	Nº	DESCRIPTION	RELEASED BY	WORK.	LOCKING	WORK	NORMAL LOCK TABLET "OUT" To.	RELEASED BY DETECTION MECHANICAL	POINT BOLTS "IN"	LOCKS
S	1.			1.						
232	2.	DOWN HOME.	7.	2.	10. 11. 19. 21. 23.	2.			(7)	
73	3.	DOWN STARTING.	13.	3.	10.	3.	WICKHAM			
5	4.			4.						
5	5.			5.						
5	6.			6.						
212	7.	F.P.L. ON 8.		7.	8.					
212	8.	DOWN LOOP POINTS.		8.	7.					
73 · 137	9.	UP SIDING Nº 2 TO UP LINE POINTS.		9.	10. 11. 12.					
81 · 154	10.	UP SIDING Nº 2 TO DOWN LINE POINTS.	13.	10.	2. 3. 9. 11. 12.					
134	11.	UP TO DOWN LINE POINTS.		11.	2. 9. 10. 12. 13.					
186	12.	UP SIDING Nº 1 CATCH POINTS.		12.	9. 10. 11.					
203	13.	UP LOOP POINTS.		13.	11. 14.					
203	14.	F.P.L. ON 13.		14.	13.					
5	15.			15.						
5	16.			16.						
72	17.	UP LINE TO UP SIDINGS GROUND SIGNAL.	(9 OR 12)	17.	19. 21. 22.	17.		(9) OR 9. 11.		
80	18.	UP SIDING Nº 2 TO DOWN LINE GROUND SIGNAL.	10.	18.	20.	18.	WICKHAM	(10)		
138	19.	UP SIDING Nº 2 TO UP LINE GROUND SIGNAL.	9.	19.	2. 17.	19.		(9)		
155	20.	DOWN LINE TO UP SIDING Nº 2 GROUND SIGNAL.	10.	20.	18.	20.		(10)		
187	21.	UP SIDING Nº 1 TO UP LINE GROUND SIGNAL.	12.	21.	2. 17.	21.		(12)		
137	22.	UP STARTING.	8.	22.	17. (9 (9) 11 (11) 12 (12))	22.	WEST MEON			
237	23.	UP HOME.	11. 14.	23.	2.	23.			(14)	
S	24.			24.						

COMMUTATOR OF TABLET INSTRUMENT TO WICKHAM
TURNED TO TABLET "OUT" Nº 18 "FREE".

Waterloo at 9.45 a.m., stopping at several suburban stations, then Guildford and Horsham before travelling on the Petersfield-Midhurst-Pulborough line to Fareham, with a stop for photographs at Horsham. It returned on the Meon Valley line, stopping for photographs at West Meon, to Alton, Aldershot, Frimley, Farnborough and Woking arriving at Waterloo at 5.07 p.m. The fare, including a copy of the itinerary, was £1. 2s 6d[13].

In late 1955, Messrs Thomas Ward of London won the contract to dismantle the closed line and sell off reusable items: station lamps appeared outside private houses, and concrete sleepers from between Hayden Lane and Meonstoke were re-used in a jetty on the River Hamble[14]. The Station Hotel became the Meon Valley Hotel and, later, The Hurdles, a pub-restaurant.

The Goods Service

Local residents were assured of a goods service which would meet their needs, running daily on the two separated sections. At Droxford Station, the signal box was demolished in 1955 and the layout of the sidings were simplified by removing some rails, particularly at the south end of the sidings[15]. A goods train ran from Fareham, stopping at Wickham, Mislingford, to Droxford, and returning tender first to Fareham but, a year or so later, it was reduced to three days a week[16]. Until the goods service ended, all trains had a brake van at each end.

A variety of steam locomotives were seen on the line: the *Greyhound* 4-4-0, with its huge driving wheels, was still used, as well as three former London, Brighton and South Coast Railway's C2x *Vulcan* 0-6-0s, *Maunsell* U Class 2-6-0s and Riddle's *Standard* 4MT types. Tank engines, newly overhauled at Eastleigh Works, were run-

In early 1955, the PORTSMOUTH EVENING NEWS reporter and photographer visited Droxford to record the impending closure. Railway closures were still a rare commodity at the time and consequently made good copy. Of the images taken few have survived. These two were lent by Ray Stone. They depict the interior of the signal box - clearly posed - plus the guard, engine crew and station master (?), names were unfortunately not given.

13. *The Railway Magazine*, Notes and News, January 1955, p. 66. A privately chartered ramblers excursion train ran on Sunday 23 January leaving Waterloo at 9.40 a.m. After picking up passengers at Clapham Junction, Wimbledon and Surbiton, it reached its destination, West Meon Station about 11.30 a.m. and left at 6.30 p.m. on the return journey. The fare was 10s, and 10s 6d. from West Croydon via Surbiton.
14. Stone, *Meon Valley Railway*, p. 102.
15. Fereday Glenn, D., *Railway Modeller*, 'The Meon Valley Railway', May 1989, p. 228-9.
16. Stone, *Meon Valley Railway*, p. 104.

70

Bedecked with wreath, flags and headboard, 'M7' No. 30055 stands at Droxford with the last down train from Alton to Fareham, Saturday 5 February 1955. The service had been made up to four coaches necessary to accommodate the additional travellers , although it appears locally at least, there were few to notice its passing at Droxford.

Tony Harden

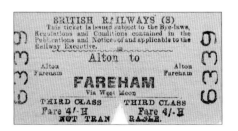

in by transporting goods and, occasionally, special passenger trains ran on the line[17].

Dr. Beeching believed the railways should be run as a business and not a public service. If parts of the railway system did not pay their way, such as some rural branch lines, they should close, the assumption being that, once unprofitable lines were closed down, the remaining system would become profitable. He ordered a study of traffic flows on all railway lines, which took place the week beginning 16 April 1962. However, the decision about the Meon Vally line had already been made.

The goods service was only busy during the sugar beet season, the Up-platform at Droxford having been strengthened to take lorries bringing beet[18]. The goods service between Fareham and Droxford failed to make a sustainable profit, and ended on 27 April 1962. Reg Gould, employed at Droxford Station for over twenty years, sadly closed and locked the station for the last time before being transferred to Botley Station for further training 'to get the grade', and then relocated to Swanwick Station. He and Doris moved from Meonstoke to Warsash[19].

In June, a locomotive brought a trainload of redundant wooden-bodied open wagons to the sidings at Droxford to be broken up[20].

17. Fereday Glenn, D.,*Railway Modeller*, 'The Meon Valley Railway', May 1989, p. 230; Fereday Glenn, D., *More . Last Days of Steam in Hampshire and The Isle of Wight,* (Stroud, 1993), pp. 90-5.
18. Grayer, Jeffrey *Railway Bylines*, 'Pacerailer Days', January 2007, p.78.
19. Mrs Doris Gould's recollections recorded by Tony Williams in October 2011.
20. Fereday Glenn, D., *More Last Days of Steam*, p. 95.

3rd Railway Correspondence & Travel Society. 3rd
Hants & West Sussex Tour
6th FEBRUARY 1955
971 971
WATERLOO, BRENTFORD, CHERTSEY
GUILDFORD, CRANLEIGH, MIDHURST
HAVANT, FAREHAM, MEON VALLEY
LINE, FARNBOROUGH, WATERLOO
(S) (S)
FOR CONDITIONS SEE OVER.

In the late afternoon sunshine of 6 February 1955, the Hampshireman special with its two steam engines, the last train to travel the full length of the Meon Valley line heads north near West Meon.

Droxford pre and post-1955. Following closure to passengers, the signal box was quickly demolished, all signals removed and the points converted to manual operation on the ground. The station name (running-in board) still survived, although who was now left to inform which station it was? This was the 'freight-only' period, to be enlivened later with a number of enthusiast special workings.

Dr J L Farmer

Droxford bound goods train passing through the Forest of Bere.
                                                    David Fereday-Glenn

A Southern 'Mogul' locomotive arrives at Droxford running tender-first from Wickham with coal and other goods. With the cessation of passenger working, the opportunity was taken to rationalise the track layout. On the right is 'Up Siding No. 1' (Mr Churchill's siding), but now connected directly into the single running line. (See original track layout plan on page 69.)
Ray Stone collection

With most private houses still using coal for heating etc, coal was a principal source of revenue for the railway well into the 1960s. The closure of various lines and wayside rail yards meant rail borne deliveries were now not always ideally placed compared with in past years - fuel previously delivered to West Meon for example now having to be collected by the merchant from Droxford. Later still British Railways would establish 'coal concentration depots' at a selected number of points, the idea being that all coal would now be delivered to just one location and either collected from there or carried by lorry in bulk to smaller distribution points - ironically the latter were often located in former railway goods yards still occupied by the actual merchants but by now devoid of rail access. For the South Hampshire area, a depot was established at Fratton. Due to the impracticalities of the idea plus a social movement away from coal towards domestic oil and gas, such 'coal concentration' yards were destined to have a short life. This is why British Railways found they had on their hands literally tens of thousands of wagons once used to carry coal but now surplus to requirements.

On this page we see the men of 'Messrs. J E Smith (Portsmouth) Ltd' unloading a wagon in Droxford yard. Work such as this was thankless, the procedure being first to open the wagon door after which a rush of coal would fall on to the ground. This would be shovelled into bags and lifted on to a waiting lorry. Next the lorry would be drawn alongside the wagon where the easier part of the procedure was now possible in that it was possible to shovel the remainder of the coal into sacks at the same height as the wagon. Some idea of the amount needing to be moved can be gauged by the carrying capacity of the wagon. The wagon had to be emptied within a set time, usually 2-3 days. Failure to do so would result in the consignee, in this case Messrs. J E Smith, having to pay a demurrage (storage) charge based on the time the wagon was not available for further use by British Railways. When loaded the hessian sacks would weight 1 cwt - note the scales under the sack in the lower view - these were then stacked lengthways on the road lorry ready for delivery.

Ray Stone collection

Shunting in Droxford yard. In the top view the guard of the train is riding on the footstep of his van, one hand used to maintain his balance and the other holding the shunting pole. At the required point, he will dismount the van to walk/run alongside the wagons and at the same time lift (release) the coupling between these with the pole. The result will be wagons placed in their required position without, hopefully, excess banging and crashing, or more importantly, injury.

In a 21st century 'Health and Safety' safety conscious world we may scoff at the idea that such practice occurred, but it must be said accidents were few, although there were always exceptions. No 'high-viz' jackets either.

In the background the contents of the open wagon cannot be determined with absolute certainty. Wooden crates are possibly the nearest guess. The van behind was originally been built for transporting animals, but it is unlikely that livestock was a regular traffic at Droxford by this time, so it may well have been used for an alternative purpose. Above both is the loading gauge: a curved piece of metal suspended on chains above one siding. Its purpose was to ensure that any wagon loaded with goods could safely pass under all bridges and tunnels on the railway system. If there was ever any doubt about the height of a load then the wagon in question would be shunted under the gauge before departure from the station. Such a simple device was commonplace on the railways until the demise of the wayside goods yard itself.

Ray Stone collection

Top - *Conversation piece at Droxford. A goods train has arrived at the station and will commence shunting shortly (At the end was engine No. 31638). North towards West Meon the track came to an abrupt end with a set of buffers. Beyond this the rails had been lifted. In the distance, the platform supports still show their wartime alternate black / white painting, the latter intended to assist passengers in the blackout but indicating also that a repaint had not been a priority since.*

Ray Stone collection

Bottom - *In June 1962, No. 30543 waits to return south having left a number of 'cripple' (defective) wagons in the yard at Droxford for storage. It is unlikely any were ever restored to use and would eventually be taken away for scrap. Nature is also rapidly reclaiming the platforms and track. By this time goods were no longer being dealt with in the yard and visits such as this were on a an occasional 'as-required' basis.*

David Fereday-Glenn

Goods train at Droxford, 28 December 1954. Notwithstanding the fact this was just after Christmas, at this time the railway still operated 365 days a year with freight a priority. Here sugar beet, a mainstay of the traffic carried on the line in latter years is being shunted. Apart from closure of the Meon Valley line in 1955, elsewhere that year would witness the announcement of the British Railways Modernisation Plan which would spell the end of the steam engine and the disastrous ASLEF strike in May / June. During this enforced stoppage much traffic was lost to road competition, never to return.

Bluebell Railway Archive / J J Smith 5-114-7

Rail enthusiasts special at Droxford, 30 April 1961. The service was the 'Locomotive Club of Great Britain' 'Solent Limited' tour. Starting from Waterloo, the route took in Portsmouth, Fareham, Droxford, Gosport, Southampton, Eastleigh Works, Newbury, Reading, Ascot and Waterloo as well as a number of changes of locomotive en-route. For the Fareham / Droxford / Gosport / Fareham leg, two tank engines, Nos. 32694 and 30200 were used.

In the top view, the train having just arrived at Droxford, the engines will shortly uncouple and then run north on to the single line before running round to recouple, as seen in the lower view, ready to depart to Fareham. Notice also the fashions of the travellers of the day, nearly all with a jacket and tie, the fashion of the period - and not an anorak to be seen! As might well be quoted decades later, 'A grand day out'.

In the lower view, local residents await the departure, unaware they are witnessing what was destined to be the final passenger train to leave Droxford.
J Courtney Haydon

One other rail enthusiasts tour had been to Droxford post 1955 and prior to the views seen on this page. This was on 7 March 1959 when a special train organised by the 'Branch Line Society' travelled up the truncated remains of the route from Fareham as part of a tour of several minor railway installations in west Sussex and south Hampshire. Post 1961, the 'Railway Correspondence and Travel Society' had advertised their 'Clausentum' railtour for 8 July 1962, this would have included a trip to Droxford but, for reasons that are not reported the trip was cancelled.

The last British Railways' goods train from Fareham to Droxford, 30 April 1962. After this time, the line would become ever more moribund with nature starting to reclaim what was once hers. But is was not to be the end, for a time much of the route would be used for the storage of redundant goods wagons - symptomatic of the decline in rail bourne freight traffic then being experienced - hundreds, nay thousands, of wagons were simply no longer required. Still to come at Droxford was the era of Mr Ashby and his railcar, plus the embryonic preservation scheme, both in the later 1960s.

D Giles

In 1973, the clerk to Droxford Rural District Council (Droxford RDC) wrote that, after closure, Droxford Station was used as a private dwelling but was no longer used for that purpose.

In May 1961, the Hampshire Narrow Gauge Railway applied to Droxford RDC about the possibility of purchasing the former railway road-bed between Droxford and West Meon, suggesting it would encourage tourism, benefiting the hotel and providing catering opportunities and, later, might lead to light engineering on a small scale. Following inconclusive negotiations with the British Transport Commission, in November 1962, they applied instead for a section of the Botley to Bishop's Waltham line.[1] In the meantime, empty wagons were stored between Droxford Station and Wickham in the summer of 1962.[2]

That autumn, Miss E. Kirkpatrick of Box Cottage, Station Road, Soberton organised a petition. She and others complained of having to look out from their homes at hundreds of wagons, and local villages protested to Droxford Parish Council and the South-East Area Planning Committee:

> We are asking for help to prevent the disfigurement of our lovely valley which is being turned in a railway rubbish dump. The trucks are blocked with sleepers to prevent movement, and so it appears to be a long-term arrangement. We hardly need to say that they look very ugly indeed, and, when the leaves have fallen from the trees, they will look worse still.

A spokesman from British Rail (BR) responded that 'These wagons are surplus to our immediate requirements and we are using the Meon Valley line as a stabling ground for them. It happens to be a convenient spot for us'.[3]

1. HRO, 78M73/DDC122.
2. Fereday Glenn, D., *Railway Modeller*, 'The Meon Valley Railway', May 1989, p. 228.
3. *Portsmouth Evening News*, 8 October 1962.

The *Pacerailer* railbus

From an unknown date, Mr Charles Sadler Ashby of the Sadler Rail Coach Company, manufacturers of rolling stock, leased part of the line running south from Droxford Station, together with the station, sidings and goods yard, to test

Above - The 'Pacerailer' at Droxford. With no available covered accommodation, a cover was erected between the existing platform canopy and the former up platform. The small diesel locomotive in the foreground was another of Ashby's purchases, used to collect items from the interchange point with British Railways at Knowle Junction. Mike Smith

a lightweight diesel railbus, the *Pacerailer*, a vehicle resembling a bus which ran on rails, and similar to the *Pacer* used at a later date by BR. He claimed that, as it had pneumatic tyres, it would be cheaper to run than a conventional train[4].

A 1-in-10 incline was constructed at the station, to test and demonstrate its potential to prospective buyers[5]. It was intended the new vehicle be compared with a steam locomotive which was brought to the station, namely an ancient Stroudley *Terrier* class A1x 0-6-0T locomotive No. 32646, and single carriage. [6]. The *Terrier* would be sold in May 1966, and delivered by road to Hayling Island to be mounted on a plinth outside the Hayling Billy Pub where it resumed its identity as a No. 46 Newington which belonged to the London, Brighton and South Coast railway.

Since the 1920s, several railway companies had tested various designs for railbuses but none were satisfactory, and were withdrawn. They could not meet passengers' expectations: the four wheels and inadequate suspension resulted in passengers having to cling to their seats to avoid being thrown about. Freight could not be hauled at the rear, while they were considered too light to operate track circuits effectively and had insufficient power to cope with loads or to take gradients.

Despite this history, Charles Ashby established the Sadler Rail Coach Company in 1963 to develop the *Pacerailer* using a body built by Strachans of Hamble, based on one of their luxury road coaches. With blue and grey livery, it was 43 ft long, 9 ft wide and 9 ft 6 inches high, with a 20 ft wheelbase, providing 50 first class seats or 75 standard seats. The driver was sited in the middle of one end. The open saloon for passengers had 'auto-air temperature control', with large windows, reclining seats, folding steps to cope with low station platforms, emergency window exits, fluorescent lighting and space for prams and parcels. Innovative at the time, a public address system gave passenger information, an automatic ticket machine took money, issued tickets and gave change, and the driver was in radio contact with signal boxes and other *Pacerailers* to ensure safe crossing on single line track.

It ran on four wheels with resilient pneumatic tyres between the hub and rim, to reduce noise levels, and self-levelling air suspension. Weighing six tons unladen, it was powered by a 9 litre AEC diesel engine designed to reach a maximum speed of 70 mph at nine miles a gallon. Ashby estimated that future production models would cost £7,500 each[7].

In 1967, there was a plan to re-open the line between Cowes and Ryde on the Isle of Wight, using railbuses, known as Vectrail. As part of this scheme, a prototype *Pacerailer* railbus in Vectrail livery, was undergoing trials at Droxford Station.[8] Lord Mountbatten, as Governor of the Isle of Wight (IOW), sat in one of its seats for a few minutes at the Island Industrial Fair at Ryde in June 1967 and expressed his opinion that it had an application for all unproductive railway lines, not just on the Isle of Wight: 'All they are doing at present is to put more buses on the roads. If this helps put buses on railway lines instead of on the road, it will be a great boon'.

Vectrail acquired rolling stock and negotiated with BR on a price for the track on the IOW, and Ashby made an application to the Isle of Wight Council in

Opposite - With apologies for the image having been used in other publications. This remains the only known colour view of the 'Pacerailer' vehicle, also referred to as the Sadler Vectrail. Based around a road coach body but running on rails, it was hoped the reduced operating costs of such a vehicle could mean otherwise unremunerative railway lines might be retained. The railbus idea had been tried by British Railways earlier, and failed, not because of the vehicle type being used but because the cost of maintaining the infrastructure around which the vehicle would operate was not covered by the revenue generated. Without a subsidy, the idea was doomed to failure from the start. Regarding the actual 'Pacerailer', one question that has never been satisfactorily answered is how it might be driven from either end? For whilst the window layout would indicate it was intended as such, there were in fact driving controls at one end only - possibly this was the prototype. The view shows the vehicle on the up platform at Droxford - next stop West Meon, unfortunately not. Although not confirmed, the man in the boiler suit may be the reclusive Mr Ashby.

Doug Hannah

4. http://www.youtube.com/watch?v=j25jhdzk7fw
5. Stone, R.A., *The Meon Valley Railway*, (Southampton, 1983), p. 106. There is no record of the *Pacerailer* having been patented in the UK.
6. Fereday Glenn, D., *More Last Days of Steam in Hampshire and The Isle of Wight,* Stroud 1993, p. 93.
7. Jeffery Grayer, *Railway Bylines*, 'Pacerailer Days', January 2007, p.78-80.
8. http://www.subbrit.org.uk/sb-sites/stations/m/merstone/index.shtml

Ashby's intended steam comparison, No. 32646 dating from the 19th century which was married to a former Bulleid design restaurant car - the latter apparently used by him as an office. Whilst the 'Pacerailer' made a number of trips south along the line it is not known if the steam engine and carriage were ever used by him. No. 32646 would survive, although the coach, itself an historic item, was broken up at Wickham some years later.

March 1969. Its Transport Committee, and a parliamentary committee, looked at the company's ability to deliver, being concerned about the small amount of capital available to the company. Mr Ashby promised to finance it himself which eventually satisfied the Transport Committee but not the Council's Works and Properties Committee who set a deadline of 30 June 1970, Mr Ashby having telephoned the County Treasurer to explain that he had separated from Vectrail and set up his own company. Called Sadler Railways Ltd, he said he had agreement with BR to purchase the line. On 10 July the committee, still having not received the necessary information, decided not to develop the

Cowes-Ryde line and to consider alternative plans. The project came to nothing, and failed to interest BR and to get any financial backing[9] .

Droxford Station

In March 1966, the British Railways Board proposed the sale of the light railway at Droxford Station to Mr Ashby for 'test and demonstration purposes', i.e. the testing of rail coaches, subject to the British Railways Board (Meon Valley) Light Railway Order (LRO) being granted by the Minister of Transport. [10]. This would enable the line to be transferred to Ashby so that he could run his project independent of BR. The light railway would extend from 148 yards north of the signal box at Knowle Junction to a point immediately south-west of the bridge where Old Winchester Hill Lane crossed the railway at West Meon Station. The draft Order was published on 31 March 1966 but it was not until 13 April 1973 that the Secretary of State made the Order, which came into operation the following day[11].

According to Jeffery Grayer, 'Although denied by BR, the Ministry of Transport drew the conclusion, probably correctly, that BR just wanted to get shot of the maintenance responsibility for the whole length. So the re-opening of the West Meon section was never on the cards'.

With objections to the Order from the National Union of Farmers and Hampshire County Council, a public enquiry was held at Petersfield on 14 November 1968. Mr Ashby settled the Union's fears by explaining that he had spent £5,000 over three years maintaining trackside fencing in the stretch where he operated and, in return for a reduction in the price of the length of track, agreed to maintain the whole section. He said that the Ministry of Technology visited Droxford in October 1968 and agreed that his work was of 'national importance', and were willing to give a grant of £10,000 towards the cost of preparing the test track: it would be relaid to provide gradients.

The chairman of the enquiry suggested the LRO be restricted to 4½ miles of track which Mr Ashby required, from Droxford Station to Bridge No. 12 about two miles north of Wickham, having contacted the Ministry of Technology who stated that Mr Ashby had not been offered any definite funding, but grants of up to 50 per cent of the cost of development would be available once he submitted a firm proposal, which he had not done. Moreover, they did not see the project

9. Grayer, 'Pacerailer Days', pp. 80-1.
10. HRO, 78M73/DDC122.
11. *The London Gazette*, 15 March 1966, p. 2862; 1 May 1973, p. 5470

An early 1960s view of the station forecourt during Mr Ashby's tenure. The giveaways are of course the motor vehicles, the two Minis - a splash of modernity against the other older designs. On the building, the poster boards remain although now devoid of information to any intending passengers. (Not thought to relate directly to Droxford is the story of the passenger in those pre-computer days who wished to travel to a rural station some hundreds of miles from his starting point. He duly purchased his ticket and, after a number of changes, eventually arrived at his last supposed changing point. Upon enquiring as to where he might board his final connection, he was politely told, "There have been no trains on that line for several years.....", the actual route having closed but that information had not found its way throughout the network.)

Tony Williams collection

as being of 'national importance'. Despite this new information, Mr Ashby still intended to operate the LRO on the 4½ miles of track[12].

Meanwhile, in November 1967, Hampshire County Council was negotiating the purchase of the disused line for road improvements to the A32, from Mr Ashby, who had contracted to buy the land from BR[13]. He reached agreement with BR in November 1969 over the terms of the sale. Hampshire County Council offered to buy the whole 10½ miles and to lease back to Mr Ashby the section he required for the LRO for seven years, at a rent of £250 a year.[14] The Order for the LRO came into operation on 14 April 1973.

Road traffic had steadily increased, and a sub-committee of Hampshire County Council had visited Droxford Station on 21 June 1968, as part of their plan to construct a road along the former railway line. Where part of the river bank had caved in on an embankment, the engineer reported that it would be possible to divert the river and take the road away from a row of houses, leaving the embankment as a barrier to keep the sound away. Forty members of the local preservation society were present: it claimed that, while Droxford would benefit, Soberton would suffer by constructing the road, as it would pass eighty-six houses and reduce their value. Local residents, mainly from Soberton, including people in Station Road, wrote letters of complaint against the scheme.

In 1965, the Southern Locomotive Preservation Society approached Mr Ashby who agreed to store their stock, including wagons and locomotives, at Droxford Station. Perhaps the Society's long-term hope was that the remaining line might be re-opened? The largest locomotive, the *USA 0-6-0T No. 30064* tank engine rescued from Salisbury motive power depot, arrived in January 1969. There was a fire in 1968 and, soon after, vandalism began, including the theft of batteries, and damage to the *Pacerailer* and other vehicles. Points were jammed and debris left on the track in an attempt to cause a derailment. The *Pacerailer* was broken into and, on 4 May 1970, it was severely damaged by fire. Rumours spread: was it an accident or arson, one suggestion being that a bus company on

12. Grayer, 'Pacerailer Days', pp. 81-2.
13. HRO, 78M73/DDC122.
14. Grayer, 'Pacerailer Days', p.82.

the Isle of Wight wanted to prevent the *Pacerailer* being introduced there.

With various prominent railway preservation groups supporting a proposal to create a preservation centre on the Longmoor Military Railway near Liss, there was less support for a similar project on the former Meon Valley Railway Line. When BR decided to close Knowle Junction, the Southern Locomotive Preservation Society moved their stock to Fareham in January 1969, and then to Liss[15]. Prior to this, for a short time, Mr Ashby had an agreement to use two small *Ruston-Hornsby* diesel shunters together with his own coach and one belonging to the SLPS to operate private charter trains on the line[16].

Hampshire County Council acquired the Meon Valley Railway Line from BR in September 1972, proposing to use the northern part of the line as a road, to reduce road traffic congestion through Droxford. The central section, between Droxford Station and Bridge No. 12 where the track remained, was leased to the Sadler Rail Coach Company for £250 a year and, on 8 January 1973, the Clerk of Hampshire County Council wrote to Droxford RDC that Droxford Station was included in the lease, for use as offices, workshops etc. The lease of the line, from Droxford to Mislingford Station, which included responsibility for its day to day maintenance, would expire in 1976[17].

New excavations

When the site of the station was constructed, one cutting was made to take the rail track, station buildings and sidings, and another for the new Station Road. High between the two cuttings, a narrow strip of land, about 100 metres long, to the south of the station building, remained untouched.

This page - The Southern Locomotive Preservation Society USA class steam locomotive No. 30064 on a weed-free track at Droxford. The Society would hold regular open days when they would give rides in their pre-served coach in the direction of Wickham. In the lower view is the shell of the dismantled former Bulleid restaurant-car.

Southern Images.

15. Stone, *Meon Valley Railway*, p. 106; Jeffrey Grayer, *Railway Bylines*, 'Pacerailer Days', January 2007, p.79, p. 82.
16. http://forum.keypublishing.com/showthread.php?p=1241275
17. HRO, 78M73/DDC122

Preserved diesel locomotive and coach in the yard at Droxford, 4 February 1967.

David Wigley

With 'Churchill's siding' on the left, a steam open day sees No. 30064 and coach leaving Droxford on 1 September 1968 about to pass under Cutts Arch Bridge. This was one of the last steaming days at Droxford as the society had vacated the site by the end of January 1969.

David Wigley

In 1970, Mr Ashby widened the platform by cutting back into the west side of this strip. No discoveries were reported at the time but, in 1973, somebody carefully examined the exposed chalk face which was eroding, and identified two graves and an iron spearhead. Because of the erosion and the implied threat to the site, the Department of the Environment and the Hampshire County Museum Service were approached, which led to part of the cemetery being excavated in July and August 1974.

Limited by the railway cutting to the west, and vegetation and service poles to the east, forty-one graves were excavated, containing over 380 objects; two other probable graves which underlay the eastern side of the excavation at the south end, were not touched. Because of the difficulty in storing the topsoil which would be returned to its original site, only an area 50 metres long at the southern end of the strip was excavated. About five hundred square yards of topsoil was removed, to a depth of about 40cm metres. When excavated, the graves, dug into the chalk to a depth varying from 10cm to 75cm, with the overlying top soil up to 50cm deep, were filled with a mixture of clay, chalk and flint.

Excavating began at the northern end, working southwards, each grave taking about four working days to excavate, record, photograph and remove the contents. Of the forty-one graves, twelve were probably male, twenty-one probably female and six juveniles or infants, while two could not be identified. Nearly half of the forty-one appear to have died between the ages of twenty and forty, of which about fourteen died before the age of twenty-five. Eight skeletons appeared to be have been under the age of twenty at death. After the age of thirty, there was a reduction in the number of females dying.

Apart from one female and three male graves which were in a north-south direction, the remaining thirty-seven lay in an east-west direction and appeared to have been in groups of up to six graves. There may have originally been a formal layout, with marker posts later destroyed by ploughing and the removal of topsoil. Evidence suggested that the graves were either left open or covered by planking, with mounds of earth on top, until the bodies and some items decayed. Two graves showed evidence of planking. As one of the four graves lying in a north-south direction appeared to have been partly dug over a grave lying in an east-west direction, it was thought that the north-south graves may have been later in date.

Thirty-two graves contained associated objects, which generally included a domestic knife from the fifth or sixth century. Five firesteels were found, used to produce a spark to light tinder by striking an iron edge with a flint, in two female graves, a child's grave and a male's. (Illustration page 20.)

Male Burials

Six male burials were each accompanied by one or more weapons, and a shield. Forty spearheads and twelve shield bosses were found, but only seven spearheads and three shield bosses were still within the original graves. The shields were thought to have been initially placed over the chest, and moved when the grave was backfilled once the body and some grave goods had decayed. The spear was normally laid alongside the body, the surviving spearhead being found on one side of the skull or upper arm.

All appeared to be from the late fifth to early sixth century, apart from one spearhead which may have been from the late sixth to early seventh century In one group, there were three warrior graves. No swords were found in 1974, but Dale had found six, five of which were examined but none indicated warriors of 'exceptionally high status'.

Female Burials

Six of the female graves contained one or more iron rings, originally attached to bags containing a variety of articles including iron, bronze and one bone/ivory rings which would have been worn, and may have been amulets. Brooches, buckles and belt mounts were found. The brooches were usually placed one on each shoulder, holding clothing in place. In five female graves, there were 213 beads, of which 159 were of amber, and the rest of glass or shale, which had been necklaces. In three of these graves, there were only five or nine beads, but a fourth had 29 beads, and the fifth 163 beads.

An almost complete long-boss style pot, from the first half of the sixth century, was found in a grave, similar to objects found at Buriton and at Little Wilbraham in Cambridgeshire. It was described as

> . . . fine, sandy, tempered with chopped straw or grass, and flint. Below the shoulder the body is divided, by nine long bosses pushed out from inside, into triangular panels each stamped with a three legged 'swastika' and vertical tooled lines.

It was found in the grave of a skeleton of a female who was about 1.55 metres (5 ft 1 in.) tall, and aged about 30 to 35 years when she died. Her grave contained a pair of identical gilt-bronze saucer brooches, and a pin, brooch, buckle and pin, tag, tube and lump all in bronze. There was an iron ring, which probably belonged to a bag which held a knife, a latch-lifter key, an object 130 mm long, up to 18 mm wide and 3 mm thick with the remains of two prongs at the wider end, and a ring, all in iron.

Close by was a grave containing the partial skeleton of a juvenile, possibility between the age of 5 to 10 years, with an iron knife by the left hip, and a bronze and iron firesteel pouch with an iron knife on the left side. These two graves lay on an east-west line. Another grave, probably made later, lay on a north-south line across the east end of the juvenile's grave, containing the skeleton of an adult male about 1.80 metres (5 ft 11 in.) in height, with a spearhead, knife, rivet or stud, and a buckle with a plate and pin, all made of iron.

Aldsworth suggested that the graveyard may have extended from 'somewhere in the vicinity of the station [building] . . . as far south as the old field boundary south of the station . . . and at least part of the way across the area subsequently occupied by the railways sidings'. Given that eight of the forty-one graves contained spearheads, and if this was typical of the cemetery, 'there must originally have been at least two hundred graves represented by the forty spearheads so far recovered'. There could be at least another hundred graves immediately north of the area excavated in 1974 and in the area immediately west of the railway cutting, giving a possible total of three hundred or more.

As at Droxford Station, many of the known pagan Saxon cemeteries in Hampshire overlooked major river valleys. Aldsworth concluded that it seemed likely that in Hampshire, as in Sussex, pagan Saxon cemeteries were sited on the boundaries of territorial areas which were mainly defined by major river valleys and water courses. Later, these areas were subdivided to form late Saxon estates, many of which eventually became parishes and Hundreds. The cemetery at Droxford Station was very close to the River Meon, the boundary between the parishes of Droxford and Soberton as well between the Domesday Hundreds of Waltham and Meonstoke.[18]

Taking up the line

It is unclear as to when Charles Ashby stopped using the line. In the early 1970s, a make-shift awning was attached to the station canopy, and two industrial diesel engines were occasionally moved while remaining stock was gradually sent elsewhere. He died in February 1976.[19]

His lease was due to end in 1976 but the line south of Wickham was probably lifted in 1974, and the section between Wickham and Droxford in 1975.[20] The Sadler Rail Coach Limited, Rail Riding Developers, went into liquidation in December 1976.[21] A meeting was held in Southampton by the liquidators, in August 1977, to report on how the Company had been wound up.[22]

From around this time a heavy goods vehicle training company took over the station and for about five years it was used as a centre for HGV driver training, this resulted in most of the Droxford station site being tarmaced. Training ceased in the early 1980s.

Hampshire County Council eventually purchased the line between West Meon and Knowle to create the Wayfarers Walk, a nature walk, which passes to the west of the former goods yard.

Right - *Ray Stone (rear) and Charles Ashby enjoy a ride along the remains of the Meon Valley line between Wickham and Droxford in 1969, possibly the last time a rail vehicle would ever travel on the line.* *Ray Stone collection*

18. Aldsworth, F., *Proceedings of the Hampshire Field Club and Archaeological Society*, 'Droxfield Anglo-Saxon Cemetery, Soberton, Hampshire', vol. 35, 1979, pp. 93-182.
19. Grayer, 'Pacerailer Days', p. 82. A Movietone film about the *Pacerailer* is included in the John Huntley 20. DVD *Classic Railway Newsreels Volume 2*. A clip of the film is on Movietone's website at www.movietone.com
20. http://en.wikipedia.org/wiki/Meon_Valley_Railway
21. *The London Gazette*, 21 December 1976, p. 17137. Its registered office was at 3 Elmfield Flats, Millbrook, Southampton.
22. *The London Gazette*, 21 July 1977, p. 9504.

The former station became a training centre for heavy goods vehicle drivers until Colin and Elizabeth Olford bought the site, which covered over two acres, at auction in 1984. They found it to be the only station on the line which has retained its platforms and 80 foot long canopy, as well as the original ticket hatch, wooden shelf, drawers and cupboards in the ticket office, wooden floors and the sliding doors which led from the booking hall to the platform.

The Olfords spent nearly two years restoring the derelict building, including the removal of a false ceiling in the booking hall to expose its vaulted ceiling and timbers, and uncovering the original fireplace. Extra rooms were created above the former ticket office, with an additional dormer window on the right side of the front of the building.

They dug up the tarmac forecourt, where lorries had practised, and transported it and the underlying hardcore to The Hurdles, where it was used to make a car park, in exchange for soil: it cost about £70 for the transport. Where the track once ran between the platforms, they planted a wild flower lawn, and created a pond and fern garden on the site of the signal box. Part of the former goods yard is now planted with specimen trees.

At the north end of the platforms, the Olfords built a garage and workshop, to resemble an engine shed, across the former track. Original timber work on the canopy above the platform was copied on its exterior. Inside, tiling on the edge of the platform has survived.

Tony and Jo Williams bought the former Droxford Station in 2009. Now, old railway sleepers are used to make raised vegetable beds in the former goods yard, while the signal box is rebuilt to its original external design but now as guest accommodation. Three of the railway's original lamp posts have been restored, one found in Kent and two brought back by truck from Cornwall. Work is ongoing although there are no plans to reinstate track or rolling stock.

Droxford Station House and Yard
Droxford, Hampshire

Estate agent illustration for the sale in 1984. The pagoda style lavatories have been removed.

Droxford reborn. From where wagon buffers crashed, coal was unloaded and prime ministers walked, all is once again tranquil. The extension at far right is a later addition, but has been sympathetically constructed to blend in with the original structure.

Towards Wickham. The platform lamp on the former up platform, one of a number salvaged from closed former LSWR stations. Identical ones stood on the original platforms.

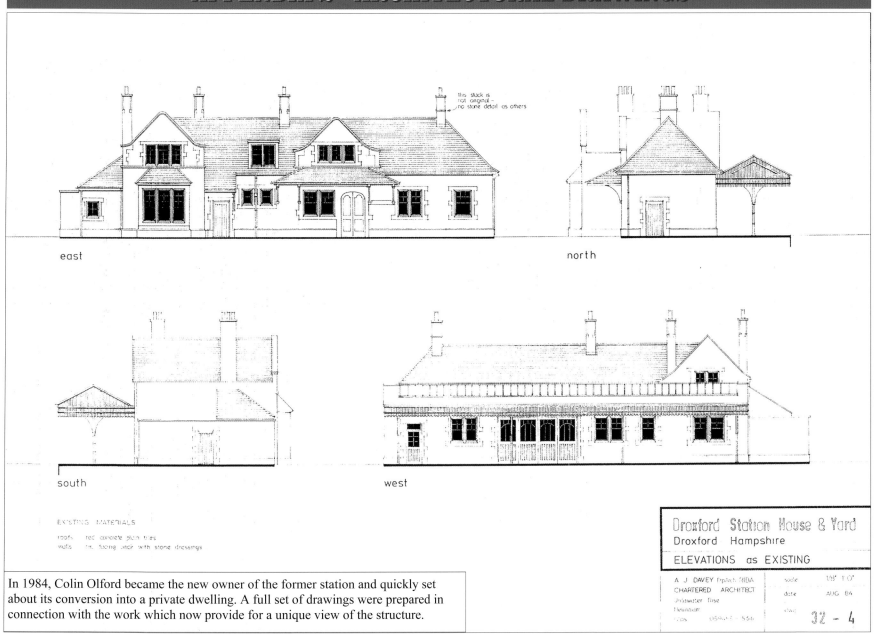

east

north

this stack is
not original –
no stone detail as others

south

west

EXISTING MATERIALS

roofs   red concrete plain tiles
walls   red facing brick with stone dressings

Droxford Station House & Yard
Droxford Hampshire

ELEVATIONS as EXISTING

A. J. DAVEY FRIBA   scale   1/8" 1'0"
CHARTERED ARCHITECT   date   AUG 84
Uplowater Rise
Newnham   dwg
Tos   0542- 556   32 - 4

In 1984, Colin Olford became the new owner of the former station and quickly set
about its conversion into a private dwelling. A full set of drawings were prepared in
connection with the work which now provide for a unique view of the structure.

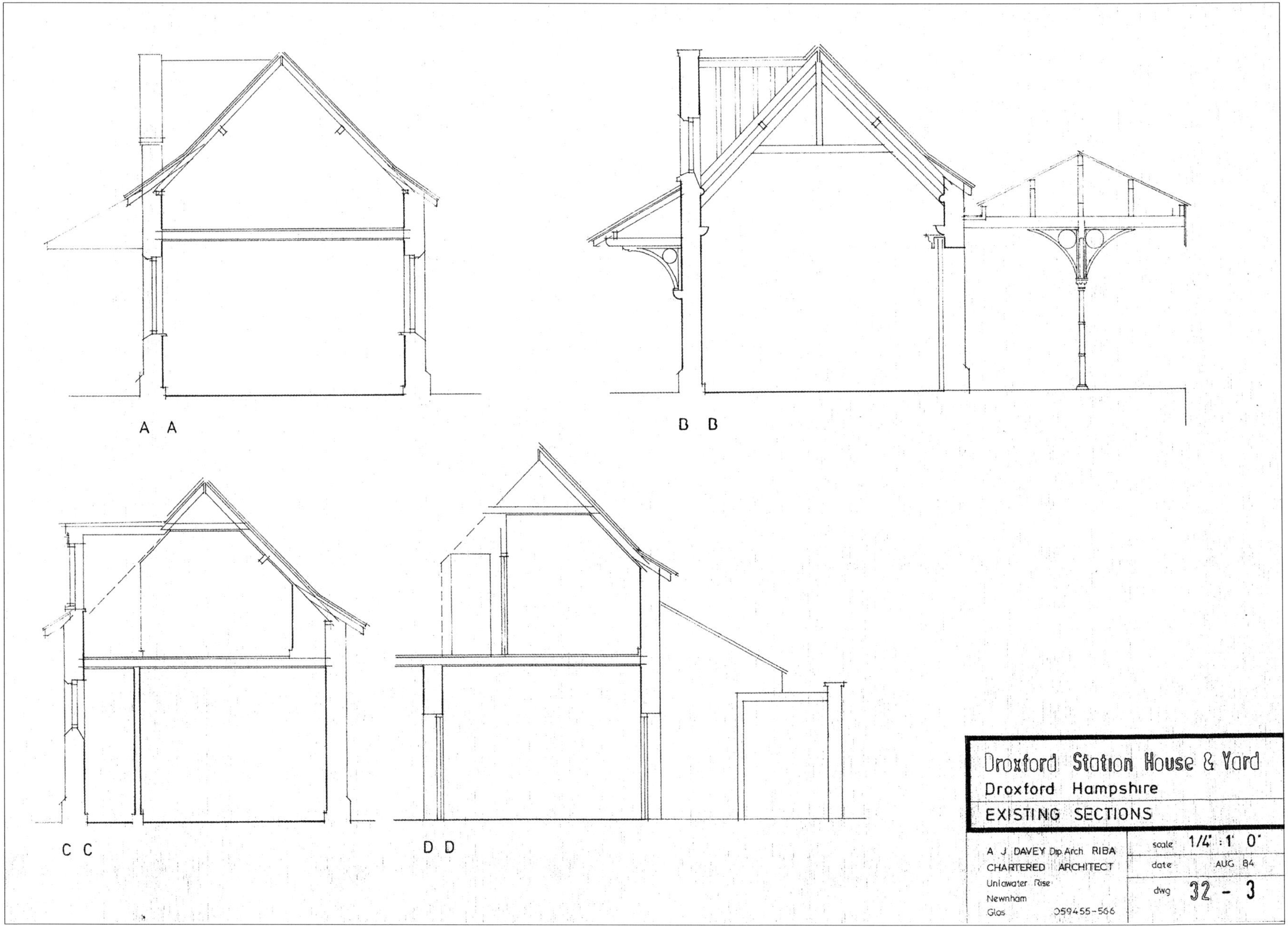

A A

B B

C C

D D

Droxford Station House & Yard
Droxford Hampshire
EXISTING SECTIONS

A J DAVEY Dip Arch RIBA	scale	1/4' : 1' 0'
CHARTERED ARCHITECT	date	AUG 84
Unlawater Rise		
Newnham	dwg	32 - 3
Glos 059455-566		

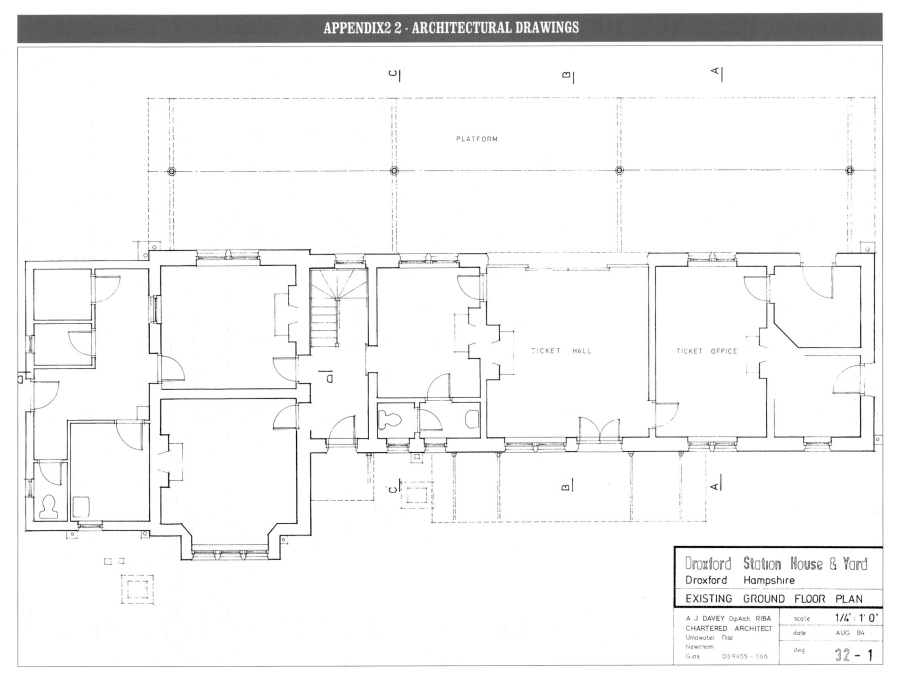

PLATFORM

TICKET HALL

TICKET OFFICE

Droxford Station House & Yard
Droxford   Hampshire

EXISTING GROUND FLOOR PLAN

A J DAVEY DipArch RIBA CHARTERED ARCHITECT Unlawater Rise Newnham G.os 059455 - 566	scale	1/4" : 1' 0"
	date	AUG 84
	dwg	32 - 1

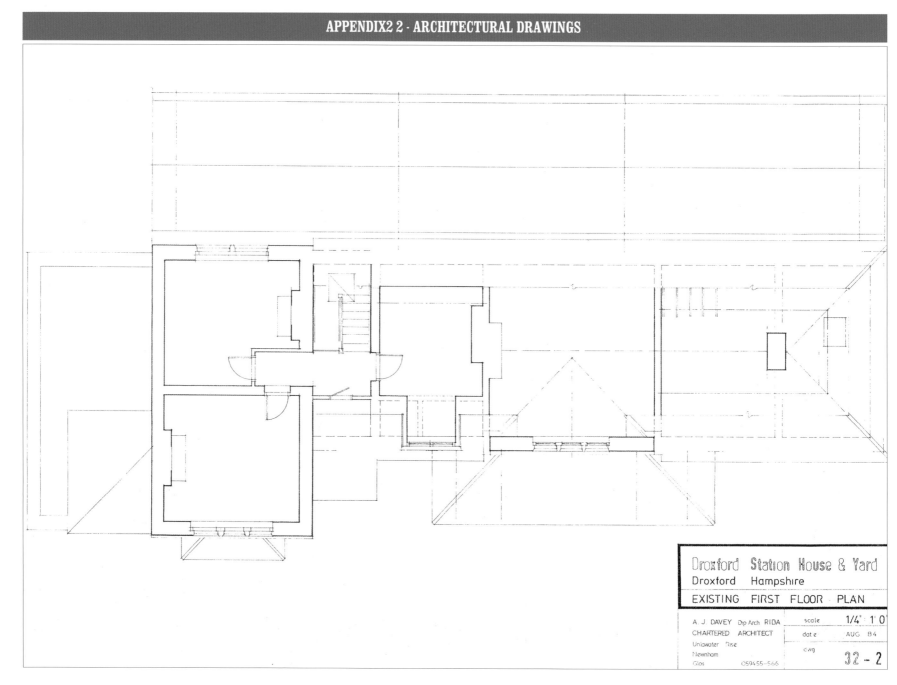

Droxford Station House & Yard
Droxford   Hampshire

EXISTING   FIRST   FLOOR   PLAN

A. J. DAVEY Dip Arch RIBA	scale	1/4" 1'0'
CHARTERED ARCHITECT	date	AUG 84
Unlawater Rise	cwg	
Newnham		32 - 2
Glos 059455-566		

Extracts from timetables, showing the departure times of trains from Droxford Station

1909, 1 June to 30 September	1914 from 7 June to 30 September	Timetable from May 1918	Timetable from 28 September 1936	Timetable from 20 September 1954
Down trains to Fareham and Gosport	Down trains to Gosport/Southampton	Down trains to Fareham	Down trains to Gosport	Down trains from Alton to Fareham
Weekdays	Weekdays	9.37 am	7.51 am	Weekdays
9.30 am	9.29 am	12.20 am	9.43 am	8.15 am (arrived at Fareham at 8.37 am)
11.45 am	11.46 am	4.21 pm	12.08 pm	9.39 am
12.33 pm	12.26 pm	7.15 pm	4.48 pm	2.04 pm
3.41 pm	3.40 pm		6.23 pm	5.03 pm
6.11 pm	6.17 pm		8.44 pm (left Waterloo at 6.39 pm)	
7.40 pm	7.39 pm (left Waterloo at 5.30 pm)		Sundays	
The last train left Waterloo at 5.30 p.m.	10.36 pm (began at West Meon)		8.57 am	
Goods trains arrive at 10.46 a.m. and leave at 11.06 a.m.	Sundays		9.04 pm	
Sundays	11.20 am			
11.21 am	8.50 pm			
8.51 pm				
Up trains to Waterloo	Up trains to Waterloo	Up trains to Alton (change at Alton for Waterloo)	Up trains to Waterloo	Up trains from Fareham to Alton
Weekdays	7.50 am (arrived at Waterloo at 10.13 am)	7.40 am	8.11 am (arrived at Waterloo at 10.24 am)	8.17 am (arrived at Alton at 8.51 am)
7.59 am (arriving at Waterloo at 10.21 am)	11.01 am	10.52 am	10.27 am	12.15 pm
10.59 am	1.56 pm	2.20 pm	1.06 pm	3.08 pm
1.56 pm	4.49 pm	6.15 pm	4.32 pm	7.08 pm
4.49 pm	6.19 pm	[There is no surviving record of a Sunday service)	7.15 pm	No Sunday Service
5.45 pm	8.00 pm		8.28 pm	
7.07 pm	10.12 pm (terminated at West Meon)		Sundays	
12.02 am	Sundays		8.39 am	
There was a Special Train for Discharged Soldiers, when required.	8.49 am		7.02 pm	
Goods trains arrive at 6.14 pm and leave at 6.35 pm.	7.44 pm			
Sundays				
8.49 am				
7.49 pm				
(Passengers had one minute to get on the train)				

		£	s	d
1898	Prelimary Fee as agreed on Contract etc,for sale	5	5	
June 27	Writing Messrs Bircham & Co, as to Title required and that it was Glebe Lands		3	6
Novr. 14	Attending them as to your Letter wishing purchase money to be used for building Parsonage and			
	they said they should pay the money into Court and try to meet your wishes		10	
	Writing you of interview and thereon		3	6
1899				
Jany 3				
5	Writing Messrs. Bircham & Co. as to title required		3	6
9	Writing you that Messrs. Bircham & Co. want to see the certificate of your Induction to the Living		3	6
11	Writing you acknowledging certificate		3	6
	Writing Messrs. Newman & Appleby as to formal Appointment of Mr. Appleby as Surveyor and for his name			
	Perusing Draft Nomination of Surveyors fo: 14		3	6
	Copy		14	
	Perusing Draft Conveyance fo: 15		4	8
	The like Plan		15	
	Copy Conveyance fo: 15		2	6
	Copy Plan		5	
13	Writing Messrs. Bircham & Co. with Draft Conveyance and Nomination of Surveyors approved		2	6
21	Collating Conveyance		3	6
	The like Plan		3	4
	The like Nomination		1	
	Writing you as to execution of Conveyance and as to Declaration required		3	4
	Writing Messrs. Bircham & Co. in reply and as to Declaration required		5	
24	Attending you to obtain your execution of Conveyance and Nomination when on reading it over you pointed out that it did		3	6
	not provide for some of the necessary accommodation works, but you signed Nomination			
	Writing Messrs. Bircham & Co. thereon as requested and as to certificate to be produced			
	Writing them returning Draft Conveyance and Plan with additions thereto to agree with contract		10	
25	Instructions for Declaration		3	6
	Drawing fo: 6 and copy		5	
	Journey to Soberton attending Mr. Holmes (who was between 80 and 90 years and very infirm) settling same with him in-		6	8
	cluding expenses		14	
	Writing Messrs. Bircham with form of Declaration & thereon	2	2	
26	Engrossing		3	6
	Plan to annex		4	
	Journey to Soberton attending you obtaining and attesting your execution of Conveyance and for actual date of your induc-		3	6
31	tion and thence on Mr. Holmes taking Declaration by him including expenses	2	2	

Date		Description		£	s	d
Feby	1	Paid Mr. Holmes			3	6
	4	Writing Messrs. Bircham & Co that Conveyance executed and Declaration made			3	
		Writing same in reply and that we are having the Declaration stamped			5	6
	9	Stamp and stamping				6
		Writing them in reply on them having paid purchase money into Court and thereon and that we will get undertaking from you as altered and as to completion			5	
		Writing you thereon and with undertaking from you to clear outgoings up to that date for your signature			5	
		Collating Duplicate Conveyance			3	
		The like Plan			1	
	11	Writing Messrs. Bircham & Co with Original and Duplicate Conveyance as requested			5	4
	16	Writing Messrs, Newman & Appleby for information required as to Land and Tithe tax on the property sold to the Railway Co. and as your discharge of outgoings			5	
	18	Writing them in reply			3	
		Writing Messrs. Bircham & Co in reply with copy Letter from Messrs. Newman & Appleby as to Tithe and Land tax and Copy Letter to enclose			5	6
	21	Writing them in reply acknowledging Duplicate Conveyance			3	
	23	Writing you money paid into Court			3	
	28	Writing Messrs. Bircham & Co with Draft and Original Nomination and Valuation of Surveyors Vendors undertaking as to outgoings and Declaration of Mr. Holmes and attending registering			5	6
		Postage and incidentals			10	
				20	12	10
		Received by cheque of Messrs. Bircham & Co. 23rd March 1899 Gunner & Penny				

Pam Buttrey, who grew up in Hertfordshire, was a head occupational therapist working in adult mental health in South London. With an MA in English Local History from the University of Leicester, she now researches local history and house histories.

More details about Pam Buttrey, can be found at www.mcfadden-buttrey.com

Also by Pam Buttrey: **Lyss Place: Peace and Turmoil among the Gentry in Liss from 900 AD**
Cane Hill Hospital: The Tower on the Hill

With Sue Hutt: **I've Got a Job to Do! A Study of the Clubhouse Model**

With D. Meredith McFadden: **Salt & Silk, Silk & Sons**

BIBLIOGRAPHY

Published Works

Bagwell, Philip S., *The Railwaymen: the history of the National Union of Railwaymen*, (London, 1963).

Beevor, Anthony, *D Day*, (London, 2009).

Binney, M., Pearce, D., (eds.), *Railway Architecture*, (London, 1979).

Buttrey, Pam, *Lyss Place: Peace and Turmoil for the Gentry in Liss from 900AD*, (South Croydon, 2008).

Coleman, Terry, *The Railway Navvies*, (London, 1965).

Dixon, Piers, *Double Diploma, The Life of Sir Pierson Dixon, Don and Diplomat*, (London, 1963).

Eden, Anthony, *The Eden Memoirs: Volume Two: The Reckoning*, (London, 1965).

Fereday Glenn, D., *More Last Days of Steam in Hampshire and The Isle of Wight,* (Stroud, 1993).

Gelling, Margaret, *Place-Names in the Landscape*, (London, 1984, 2000 edn.).

Gilbert, Martin, *Winston S. Churchill: Volume Seven: Road to Victory 1941-1945*, vol. 7, (London, 1986).

Lewis, Samuel, *Topographical Dictionary of England*, vol. 4, (London, 1859).

Jenkinson, John A., Lamb, David R. &Travis, Charles, *Railway Operation: The Passenger Station and Signalling*, (London, 1914).

Kelly's Directory of Hampshire, Wiltshire, Dorset and the Channel Islands, 1923.

Kelly's Directory of Hampshire, Wiltshire, Dorset and the Channel Islands, 1907; *Kelly's Directory of Hampshire and the Isle of Wight*, 1915.

Oppenheimer, S., *The Origins of the British*, (London, 2006, 2007 edn.).

Proceedings of the Hampshire Field Club and Archaeological Society, vol. 35, 1979.

Robertson, Keith, *Hampshire Railways in Old Photographs*, (Gloucester, 1989).

Simmons, J., Biddle, N., (eds.), *The Oxford Companion to British Railway History*, (Oxford 1997, 1999 edn.).

Stone, R.A., *The Meon Valley Railway*, (Southampton, 1983).

The Architects & Surveyors Directory and Referendum.

The R.I.B.A. Kalendar.

Tillman, Denis, *The Meon Valley Revisited*, (Bishop's Waltham, 2003).

Victoria County History, Hampshire and the Isle of Wight, ed. W. Page, vol. 3, (London, 1908).

Ward, Kenneth, *Droxford in the Meon Valley*, (Havant).

Who's Who.

Williams, A. & Martin, G.H., eds., *Domesday Book*, (London, 2002).

Wolmar, Christian, *Fire and Steam*, (London, 2007).

Yorke, Barbara, *Wessex in the Early Middle Ages*, (Leicester, 1995).

Journals and Newspapers

Hampshire Chronicle
Portsmouth Evening News
Railway Bylines
Railway Modeller
The London Gazette
The Railway Magazine
The Times

Websites

http://en.wikipedia.org/wiki/Battle_of_the_Falkland_Islands
http://en.wikipedia.org/wiki/Doveton_Sturdee
http://en.wikipedia.org/wiki/Meon_Valley_Railway
http://forum.keypublishing.com/showthread.php?p=1241275
http://hansard.millbanksystems.com/commons/1919/jul/24/meon-valley-railway
http://janus.lib.cam.ac.uk/db/node.xsp?id=EAD%2FGBR%2F0014%2FSDEE
http://www.1911census.co.uk/search/tnaform.aspx
http://www.bbc.co.uk/ww2peopleswar/stories/46/a3394046.shtml
http://www.british-history.ac.uk/report.aspx?compid=46472
http://www.nottingham.ac.uk/english/ins/kepn/detailpop.php?placeno=6628
http://www.subbrit.org.uk/sb-sites/stations/m/merstone/index.shtml
http://www.youtube.com/watch?v=j25jhdzk7fw

CD Roms

SWC Meon Valley Portfolio

Enjoy local history?

Then more information on the Meon Valley Railway is available in this series of books.

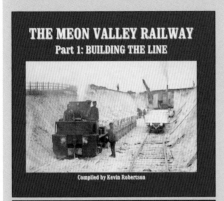

THE MEON VALLEY RAILWAY Part 1: Building the Line.

Published January 2011, this first volume explores the building of the railway with over 80 carefully selected contemporary images. A chance find led to the discovery of the collection - many miles from Hampshire - taken over a century ago by a railway 'Missionary' whose 'flock' included the navvies and their families. *"An excellent volume…." - Michael Hawkins on Amazon.*

Casebound, presented on quality art paper, 72 sides.   ISBN 978 1 906419 47 2   £14.95.

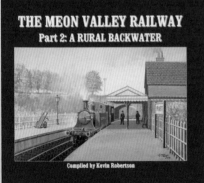

THE MEON VALLEY RAILWAY Part 2: A Rural Backwater.

Published January 2012, the second volume in the series takes the story of the railway from the time of opening in 1903 through to the issue of the closure notice for 1955. Copious illustrations, many published for the first time, describe the stations and route as well as some of the characters of the railway. There is also a 'flashback' feature with additional information supplementing the first volume. *"This book was well up to standard and well illustrated…...hurry up Part 3"* -Amazon review.

Casebound, presented on quality art paper, 84 sides. ISBN 978 1 906419 68 4   £16.95.

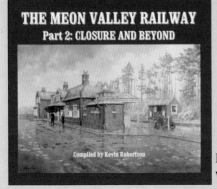

THE MEON VALLEY RAILWAY Part 2: Closure and Beyond.

Published January 2013, this final volume concludes the story of this much loved railway from the running of the last trains, to the freight only services to Farringdon and Droxford, the abortive preservation scheme and eventual demolition. Again more new information relevant to Parts 1 and 2 is included. Copious colour and b/w illustrations.

Casebound, presented on quality art paper, 84 sides. ISBN 978 1 906419 96 7   £16.95 (tbc)

Produced and printed in the UK by Noodle Books. PO Box 279, CORHAMPTON, Southampton. SO32 3ZX. www.noodlebooks.co.uk   01489 877880